Elements of Literature
Third Course

HOLT ASSESSMENT
Writing, Listening, and Speaking
Tests and Answer Key

- **Workshop Tests in Standardized Test Formats**
- **Evaluation Forms**
- **Scales and Rubrics**
- **Holistic Scoring Guides**
- **Analytical Scale: 7 Writing Traits**
- **Sample Papers**
- **Portfolio Assessment**

HOLT, RINEHART AND WINSTON

A Harcourt Education Company

Orlando • **Austin** • New York • San Diego • Toronto • London

Copyright © by Holt, Rinehart and Winston

All rights reserved. No part of this publication may be reproduced or transmitted in any form or by any means, electronic or mechanical, including photocopy, recording, or any information storage and retrieval system, without permission in writing from the publisher.

Teachers using ELEMENTS OF LITERATURE may photocopy blackline masters in complete pages in sufficient quantities for classroom use only and not for resale.

ELEMENTS OF LITERATURE, HOLT, and the "Owl Design" are trademarks licensed to Holt, Rinehart and Winston, registered in the United States of America and/or other jurisdictions.

Printed in the United States of America

If you have received these materials as examination copies free of charge, Holt, Rinehart and Winston retains title to the materials and they may not be resold. Resale of examination copies is strictly prohibited.

Possession of this publication in print format does not entitle users to convert this publication, or any portion of it, into electronic format.

ISBN 0-03-079004-2

3 4 5 6   179   07

Table of Contents

Overview of Elements of Literature Assessment Program vii

About This Book x

Writing Workshop Tests and Answer Key

Multiple-choice test for each Writing Workshop

for Collection 1
Writing Workshop: Autobiographical Narrative 3

for Collection 2
Writing Workshop: Short Story 6

for Collection 3
Writing Workshop: Analyzing Nonfiction 10

for Collection 4
Writing Workshop: Comparing Media Coverage 14

for Collection 5
Writing Workshop: Persuasive Essay 17

for Collection 6
Writing Workshop: Describing a Place 20

for Collection 7
Writing Workshop: Analyzing a Poem 23

for Collection 8
Writing Workshop: Analyzing a Short Story 27

for Collection 9
Writing Workshop: Research Paper 30

for Collection 10
Writing Workshop: Persuading with Cause and Effect 36

for Collection 11
Writing Workshop: Comparing a Play and a Film 39

for Collection 12
Writing: Business Letter 42

Answer Sheet 1 45

Answer Sheet 2 46

Answer Key 47

Table of Contents *continued*

Workshop Scales and Rubrics

Analytical scales and scoring rubrics for

- Writing Workshops
- Listening and Speaking Workshops

for **Collection 1**
    Writing: Autobiographical Narrative   Scale and Rubric 53
    Speaking: Oral Narrative   Scale.. 56

for **Collection 2**
    Writing: Short Story   Scale and Rubric 57

for **Collection 3**
    Writing: Analyzing Nonfiction   Scale and Rubric 60

for **Collection 4**
    Writing: Comparing Media Coverage   Scale and Rubric..................... 63

for **Collection 5**
    Writing: Persuasive Essay   Scale and Rubric 66
    Listening and Speaking:
        Conducting a Debate   Scale 69
        Judging a Debate   Scale 70

for **Collection 6**
    Writing: Describing a Place   Scale and Rubric 71
    Speaking: Presenting a Description   Scale.. 74

for **Collection 7**
    Writing: Analyzing a Poem   Scale and Rubric 75
    Speaking: Presenting a Poem   Scale 78

for **Collection 8**
    Writing: Analyzing a Short Story   Scale and Rubric 79

for **Collection 9**
    Writing: Research Paper   Scale and Rubric 82
    Speaking: Presenting Research   Scale 85

for **Collection 10**
    Writing: Persuading with Cause and Effect   Scale and Rubric.......... 86
    Speaking: Persuasive Speech   Scale 89

for **Collection 11**
    Writing: Comparing a Play and a Film   Scale and Rubric.................. 90
    Listening: Analyzing and Evaluating Speeches   Scale 93

for **Collection 12**
    Writing: Business Letter   Scale.. 94

Table of Contents *continued*

Scales and Sample Papers

Scales for assessing writing

Student sample papers with evaluations

Analytical Scale: 7 Writing Traits 97

Biographical or Autobiographical Narrative
    Holistic Scale 104
    Sample Papers and Evaluations... 106

Exposition
    Holistic Scale 113
    Sample Papers and Evaluations... 115

Response to Literature
    Holistic Scale 122
    Sample Papers and Evaluations... 124

Persuasion
    Holistic Scale 132
    Sample Papers and Evaluations... 134

Business Letter
    Holistic Scale 141
    Sample Papers and Evaluations... 143

Portfolio Assessment

An essay on portfolio management

Portfolio Assessment in the Language Arts 153

How to Develop and Use Portfolios 156

Conferencing with Students 165

Questions and Answers 169

Forms for evaluating writing, listening, and speaking

Portfolio Table of Contents 175
About This Portfolio 176
Home Review: What the Portfolio Shows 178
Home Response to the Portfolio 179
Writing Record 180
Spelling Log 181
Goal-Setting for Writing, Listening, and Speaking 182
Summary of Progress: Writing, Listening, and Speaking 184
Writing Self-Inventory 186

Table of Contents *continued*

Writing Process Self-Evaluation **187**
Proofreading Strategies **188**
Proofreading Checklist **189**
Record of Proofreading Corrections **190**
Multiple-Assignment Proofreading Record **191**
Listening Self-Inventory **192**
Speaking Self-Inventory **193**
Skills Profile **195**

FOR THE TEACHER

Overview of ELEMENTS OF LITERATURE Assessment Program

Two assessment booklets have been developed for ELEMENTS OF LITERATURE.

(1) Assessment of student mastery of selections and specific literary, reading, and vocabulary skills in the **Student Edition:**

- *Holt Assessment: Literature, Reading, and Vocabulary*

(2) Assessment of student mastery of workshops and specific writing, listening, and speaking skills in the **Student Edition:**

- *Holt Assessment: Writing, Listening, and Speaking*

Diagnostic Assessment

Holt Assessment: Literature, Reading, and Vocabulary contains two types of diagnostic tests:

- The Entry-Level Test is a diagnostic tool that helps you determine (1) how well students have mastered essential prerequisite skills needed for the year and (2) to what degree students understand the concepts that will be taught during the current year. This test uses multiple tasks to assess mastery of literary, reading, and vocabulary skills.

- The Collection Diagnostic Tests help you determine the extent of students' prior knowledge of literary, reading, and vocabulary skills taught in each collection. These tests provide vital information that will assist you in helping students master collection skills.

> **NOTE:** You may wish to address the needs of students who are reading below grade level. If so, you can administer the Diagnostic Assessment for Reading Intervention, found in the front of *Holt Reading Solutions*. This assessment is designed to identify a student's reading level and to diagnose the specific reading comprehension skills that need instructional attention.

Holt Online Essay Scoring can be used as a diagnostic tool to evaluate students' writing proficiency:

- For each essay, the online scoring system delivers a holistic score and analytic feedback related to five writing traits. These two scoring methods will enable you to pinpoint the strengths of your students' writing as well as skills that need improvement.

Ongoing, Informal Assessment

The **Student Edition** offers systematic opportunities for ongoing, informal assessment and immediate instructional follow-up. Students' responses to their reading; their writing, listening, and speaking projects; and their work with vocabulary skills all serve as both instructional and ongoing assessment tasks.

vii

Overview of ELEMENTS OF LITERATURE Assessment Program *continued*

- Throughout the **Student Edition,** practice and assessment are immediate and occur at the point where skills are taught.

- In order for assessment to inform instruction on an ongoing basis, related material repeats instruction and then offers new opportunities for informal assessment.

- **Skills Reviews** at the end of each collection offer a quick evaluation of how well students have mastered the collection skills.

Progress Assessment

Students' mastery of the content of the **Student Edition** is systematically assessed in two test booklets:

- *Holt Assessment: Literature, Reading, and Vocabulary* offers a test for every selection. Multiple-choice questions focus on comprehension, the selected skills, and vocabulary development. In addition, students write answers to constructed-response prompts that test their understanding of the skills.

- *Holt Assessment: Writing, Listening, and Speaking* provides both multiple-choice questions for writing and analytical scales and rubrics for writing, listening, and speaking. These instruments assess proficiency in all the writing applications appropriate for each grade level.

Summative Assessment

Holt Assessment: Literature, Reading, and Vocabulary contains two types of summative tests:

- The Collection Summative Tests, which appear at the end of every collection, ask students to apply their recently acquired skills to a new literary selection. These tests contain both multiple-choice questions and constructed-response prompts.

- The End-of-Year Test helps you determine how well students have mastered the skills and concepts taught during the year. This test mirrors the Entry-Level Test and uses multiple tasks to assess mastery of literary, reading, and vocabulary skills.

FOR THE TEACHER

Overview of ELEMENTS OF LITERATURE Assessment Program *continued*

Holt Online Essay Scoring can be used as an end-of-year assessment tool:

- You can use *Holt Online Essay Scoring* to evaluate how well students have mastered the writing skills taught during the year. You will be able to assess student mastery using a holistic score as well as analytic feedback based on five writing traits.

Monitoring Student Progress

Both *Holt Assessment: Literature, Reading, and Vocabulary* and *Holt Assessment: Writing, Listening, and Speaking* include skills profiles that record progress toward the mastery of skills. Students and teachers can use the profiles to monitor student progress.

***One-Stop Planner*® CD-ROM with ExamView® Test Generator**

All of the questions in this booklet are available on the *One-Stop Planner*® **CD-ROM with ExamView® Test Generator.** You can use the ExamView Test Generator to customize any of the tests in this booklet. You can then print a test unique to your classroom situation.

Holt Online Assessment

You can use *Holt Online Assessment* to administer and score the diagnostic and summative tests online. You can then generate and print reports to document student growth and class results. For your students, this online resource provides individual assessment of strengths and weaknesses and immediate feedback.

FOR THE TEACHER
About This Book

This book, ***Holt Assessment: Writing, Listening, and Speaking***, accompanies the ELEMENTS OF LITERATURE program and provides a variety of assessment resources. These include Writing Workshop Tests and Answer Key, Workshop Scales and Rubrics, Scales and Sample Papers, and Portfolio Assessment.

WRITING WORKSHOP TESTS AND ANSWER KEY

Every Writing Workshop in ELEMENTS OF LITERATURE has an accompanying Writing Workshop Test in a standardized test format. The test format not only will allow you to assess student performance but also will familiarize students with standardized tests and give them experience in test taking.

Each Writing Workshop Test provides a passage containing problems or errors in several or all of the following areas: content, organization, style, and conventions. Students demonstrate their understanding of the writing genre and their revising and proofreading skills by responding to multiple-choice items. Students revise elements of the genre, restructure segments of the passage, add or delete statements, refine language, and correct errors in the passage.

Answer Sheets

Answer Sheets immediately follow the tests in this section. The Answer Sheets correspond to the answer options on a particular standardized test. Use the following chart to help you determine which answer sheet to use.

Collection	Answer Sheet
Collection 1 Workshop	(answers marked on test)
Collections 2–8 and 10–12 Workshops	Answer Sheet 1
Collection 9 Workshop	Answer Sheet 2

Answer Key

The Answer Key follows the Answer Sheets at the end of this section of the book. In addition to giving the correct answer, the Answer Key tells which Workshop skill is assessed by each item.

FOR THE TEACHER
About This Book *continued*

WORKSHOP SCALES AND RUBRICS

This section contains analytical scales and scoring rubrics for Writing Workshops and scales for Listening and Speaking Workshops. Both the scales and the rubrics are important teacher evaluation tools. In addition, students can use the scales and rubrics as learning and evaluation guides for their own work.

The **scales** include essential criteria for mastery of skills and ratings of each criterion based on a four-point scale. The **rubrics** are based on the same criteria listed in the scales. The rubrics clearly describe a student's work at each score point level for each specific criterion.

Score Point 0

On occasion, student work may be unscorable and consequently will receive a score point of zero. This may be true of writing, listening and speaking, and media assignments. The following are reasons to give a product a score of zero. The work

- is not relevant to the prompt or assignment
- is only a rewording of the prompt or assignment
- contains an insufficient amount of writing (or other mode) to determine whether it addresses the prompt or assignment
- is a copy of previously published work
- is illegible, incomprehensible, blank, or in a language other than English

FOR THE TEACHER
About This Book *continued*

SCALES AND SAMPLE PAPERS — This section contains two different kinds of scales for assessing writing: the Analytical Scale: 7 Writing Traits and the individual four-point holistic scales for fictional or autobiographical writing, exposition, responses to literature, persuasion, and business letters. Accompanying these scales are high-level, mid-level, and low-level examples of student writing. Individual evaluations, based on the analytical and holistic scales, follow each sample student paper. These scales can be used for on-demand writing or class assignments. Although this section is directed to teachers, students may also benefit from access to this section as they write and revise.

PORTFOLIO ASSESSMENT — This section provides an introduction to portfolio work, including suggestions about how to develop and use portfolios and how to conduct conferences with students about their work.

Forms — The introductory article is followed by a set of student forms for assessing and organizing portfolio contents and for setting goals for future work. Also included is a set of forms for communicating with parents or guardians about student work and for generally assessing students' progress.

Forms in this section can be used to record work, to establish baselines and goals, and to think critically about student work in a variety of areas. These areas include writing, listening, and speaking. The goal of these forms is to encourage students to develop criteria for assessing their own work and to identify areas for improvement. Many forms can also be used for assessment of a peer's work and for teacher evaluations.

Writing Workshop Tests and Answer Key

for COLLECTION 1 — page 78

Writing Workshop: Autobiographical Narrative

DIRECTIONS Read the passage (which may contain some errors) and answer the questions that follow. Be sure to fill in the bubble next to the answer you choose. Mark like this ◉ not like this ⊘. You may look back at the passage as you answer questions.

The Long View

1 Like magic carpet rides, my mother's stories instantly transported me to
2 distant times and places. My mother, Carlotta Maria Paloma Chavez, was
3 born and raised on the Texas plains. I know that, as a child, she loved the
4 way she could see for great distances. Only now and then would a tree
5 pierce the sky, showing up at a great distance. "Otherwise," she would say,
6 "you could see forever." She called it "seeing the long view."

7 Every now and then when life became too hard or lonely, my mother
8 would look at me and say, "Let's go see the long view." Then the two of us
9 would take off for the afternoon and ride the Staten Island Ferry. On the
10 ferry we were not held in by New York's barriers of buildings. Sometimes
11 as we rode the ferry my mother talked about her life in Texas. For a few
12 hours at least, the boat was a place where we forgot our problems while
13 enjoying the fresh smells of the sea and the harsh calls of the gulls.

14 The cost of the ride matched our pocketbooks. There's an old saying that
15 you get what you pay for. In the case of the Staten Island Ferry, we got
16 much more. Many people prefer the efficiency of planes, trains, and cars,
17 but I prefer the experience of a leisurely boat ride.

18 Few other places can bring back the sheer pleasure that my mother and I
19 experienced on our ferry rides. The trip from Manhattan to Staten Island
20 gave us a fresh, new outlook on life. Seeing the beautiful skyline of lower
21 Manhattan and the big figure of the Statue of Liberty made us forget the
22 petty things that had been wearing us down. The ride worked its same
23 magic on the big problems, the ones that sometimes felt too overwhelming
24 to solve. Those rides let us see the long view and the city.

GO ON

for **COLLECTION 1** continued

AUTOBIOGRAPHICAL NARRATIVE

1 Which of the following words hint at the meaning of the experience?

○ My mother, Carlotta Maria Paloma Chavez (line 2)
○ raised on the Texas plains (line 3)
○ she could see for great distances (line 4)
○ seeing the long view (line 6)

2 In the sentence, *Only now and then would a tree pierce the sky, showing up at a great distance*, which of the following would be the BEST change to the underlined phrase?

○ breaking the view of barren land
○ showing the edge of the plains
○ breaking the limitless horizon
○ breaking out of nowhere

3 Which of the following sentences, if added in line 9, would BEST explain the narrator's feelings?

○ The ferry's motors and their wake churned the harbor water.
○ Once on the boat, we were no longer alone or weary.
○ I can still recall the panorama of the huge city.
○ My mother told me some of her fondest memories on those outings.

4 Which sentence could BEST be added before the last sentence in paragraph 2 to convey the narrator's feelings?

○ Birds circled the boat searching for handouts from generous tourists.
○ Sometimes my friends also enjoy outings away from the city.
○ The long views, out on the water, were soothing.
○ Many sightseers on the ferry had not previously visited New York.

5 Which of the following sentences could BEST replace the last sentence of paragraph 3?

○ We enjoyed getting away from the city noise, vehicle emissions, and busy people.
○ The ride lasted a long time and felt like a break from daily chores.
○ The cost of the ferry has always been low, but, since July 4, 1997, the ride has been free.
○ When I listened to her stories, my mother's memories of open spaces seemed like fantasies.

6 Which of the following phrases could be added after *the harsh calls of the gulls?* (line 13)

○ and the brisk breeze in our hair
○ and tourists all around us
○ and hot, humid summer air
○ and the roll of the boat

7 Which of the following phrases BEST explains the narrator's reflection on what was learned?

○ matched our pocketbooks (line 14)
○ you get what you pay for (line 15)
○ fresh, new outlook on life (line 20)
○ felt too overwhelming (line 23)

8 What was the actual order of events?

○ The writer was ferried between New York and Texas.
○ Carlotta Chavez lived in New York and then moved to Texas.
○ Carlotta Chavez was born in Texas and moved to New York.
○ The writer was born in Texas and moved to New York.

GO ON

4 Holt Assessment: Writing, Listening, and Speaking

for **COLLECTION 1** continued

AUTOBIOGRAPHICAL NARRATIVE

9 Which of the following would be the BEST change?

- ○ Change **figure** to **sight** (line 21)
- ○ Change **big** to **valiant** (line 21)
- ○ Change **petty** to **small** (line 22)
- ○ Change **problems** to **things** (line 23)

10 Which of the following phrases is preferable to *the city* in line 24 in order to reveal the significance of the experience?

- ○ work on the ferry
- ○ rediscover what was important to us
- ○ the important views that were there
- ○ the buildings of New York

Writing Workshop: Short Story

for COLLECTION 2 *page 154*

DIRECTIONS Pam's teacher has asked students to write a short story. Pam is writing a short story based on a meaningful experience in her life.

Here is Pam's draft.

Our expectations were high.(1) Students were sitting in the front row(2) of the auditorium. Mr. Garza, the school's drama teacher, had called a(3) meeting of the cast and crew to talk about costumes for our class play.

"I'm thinking about a royal blue gown for the ballroom scene," Lisa(4) whispered.

"I want a gold one," came my reply.(5)

One of the best rewards for our hard work would be the fun of waltzing(6) onto the stage wearing beautiful, brightly colored costumes. Then, with just(7) a few words, Mr. Garza took away that dream.

"Our department budget won't stretch far enough to buy new(8) costumes," he announced. "You'll have to make do with those we have(9) in the property room."

"There goes the gold!" I thought.(10)

Lisa and I volunteered to go look at the old clothes while the others(11) began rehearsals. Mr. Garza handed us the key, and we headed for what(12) we called "the dungeon." It's a large room crammed full of furniture,(13) clothes, dishes, and anything else that had been or could be used for our plays.

"This stubborn door is stuck," Lisa complained as she turned the key(14) and pushed.

The costume racks were against the back wall, so we had to make our(15) way around piles of dust-laden objects.

"Some of this stuff is really old," I said, drawing a streak in the dust on(16) an end table.

GO ON

Then I noticed a large drawer resting under its marble top. I was surprised to see a thick notebook inside. I carefully lifted it out and opened it. Attached to the inside cover was a program from 1951 announcing the same play that we were doing.

"What a coincidence!" I remarked.

"Yes, and we'll probably have to wear the same costumes they used more than fifty years ago," Lisa replied.

As we thumbed through the notebook, we were transported back in time. A student named Dora Mae Brown had documented every detail of the 1951 production. Their experience was very similar to ours – except for one big difference. Below a large photograph of the cast, Dora Mae had written how hard everyone had worked for the beautiful costumes they wore.

The students had worked to earn money to buy the material. Then they had "costume parties" to make both the boys' and girls' outfits. Students, parents, and even some teachers helped.

Regretting our selfishness, Lisa and I easily found the costumes shown in the photograph. As we sorted through the timeworn garments, the old clothes seemed to come alive. Although faded with age and some loose at the seams, they were beautiful and showed evidence of meticulous hand stitching and beadwork. Even the boys' fancy waistcoats had been hand sewn.

With notebook in hand and armloads of ball gowns, we left the storage room. When we proposed having our own "costume party" to restore the old clothes, everyone laughed at our newfound meaning for the term.

for COLLECTION 2 continued — SHORT STORY

1 In sentence 2, what should Pam do to better identify the narrator?

   A Change the word "Students" to "My friend Lisa and I."
   B Begin the story by explaining the plot of the play.
   C Tell about the character she would be in the play.
   D Leave as is.

2 What narrative details could BEST be added right before sentence 6?

   A All my classes were interesting, but also required lots of time-consuming homework.
   B We had been through nerve-wracking tryouts, long rehearsals, and tedious set building.
   C Rehearsals were held after school and usually lasted until dinnertime.
   D After rehearsals, cast members sometimes ordered pizza and talked for hours before heading home.

3 In sentence 7, which verb would BEST replace "took away"?

   A revised
   B realized
   C answered
   D shattered

4 Which sensory details should Pam add to the end of sentence 10?

   A remembering some athletes' feelings during the Olympic competitions
   B changing my mind about the color I wanted to wear for the ballroom scene
   C feeling my stomach twist with a sharp pang of disappointment
   D keeping my thoughts to myself so the others would not be unhappy

5 Which word or phrase could Pam add at the beginning of sentence 11 to BEST help develop the main characters?

   A Also,
   B Seeking sympathy,
   C However,
   D Although devastated,

6 In sentence 12 before the word "headed," which word would BEST express the internal conflict?

   A quietly
   B grudgingly
   C secretly
   D proudly

7 To describe the setting, which sentence should be added after sentence 14?

   A I was a little frightened about what we might find.
   B Lisa was dramatic, even when she was not performing on the stage.
   C Finally, it opened, and the room breathed a musty sigh of relief.
   D We spent almost ten minutes wandering through the prop room.

GO ON

for COLLECTION 2 continued

SHORT STORY

8 Which chronological event should Pam provide right after sentence 17?

  A Lisa and I looked at each other and smiled.

  B Curious, I pulled open the drawer.

  C I wondered if the table were an antique.

  D The table was desperate for a good coat of polish.

9 What sentence would BEST add to the order of events after sentence 34?

  A I was delighted to have found a wearable ball gown.

  B Mr. Garza was pleased that we had made a thorough inventory.

  C Lisa and I wanted to keep the notebook contents a secret.

  D We hurried to show the others what we had found.

10 What should Pam add to the end of her story?

  A more information about the narrator

  B a short summary of the narrative details

  C a sentence related to the story's theme

  D a vivid description of the costumes that they found

Writing Workshop: Analyzing Nonfiction

DIRECTIONS Charlene's teacher has asked students to write an analysis of a biography. Charlene is writing an essay in which she will analyze *Mae Jemison: A Space Biography*, by Della A. Yannuzzi. Here is Charlene's draft.

Note: Charlene has not yet added the citations that refer to pages in the biography.

Mae Jemison: Charting Her Own Course

In *Mae Jemison: A Space Biography*, the author portrays Jemison as an (1) extraordinary woman whose quest for personal achievement has led her to success. Mae Jemison is the first African American woman astronaut, (2) but that is only part of her remarkable life.

Yannuzzi suggests that the setting in which Jemison grew up helped (3) nurture her talents. Her parents, Charlie and Dorothy Jemison, valued (4) education highly. In 1959, when Jemison was three, they moved the family (5) from Decatur, Alabama, to Chicago, Illinois. They wanted to make sure that (6) their three children received a better education than the segregated schools of the South offered African Americans. Jemison's parents encouraged her (7) interest in science, which was then considered a nontraditional career choice for women—particularly women of color. Yannuzzi recounts how, (8) when Jemison told her kindergarten teacher that she wanted to be a scientist when she grew up, the teacher responded, "You mean a nurse, don't you?" Nevertheless, at home she was allowed the freedom (9) to pursue her natural interests and thinking for herself.

Jemison's determination propelled her toward her achievements. She (10) (11) became even more fascinated with science as she grew older. She avidly (12) studied books on astronomy, and closely followed developments in the space program. The author demonstrates that Jemison learned to shape (13) events rather than wait for them to happen. Once, for a science fair project, (14) she contacted a local hospital for information on sickle cell anemia.

GO ON

10 Holt Assessment: Writing, Listening, and Speaking

for **COLLECTION 3** continued

ANALYZING NONFICTION

Before long, she had a part-time job in the hospital's lab, supplementing (15) her science courses with practical experience. After winning a National (16) Achievement Scholarship, she went on to Stanford University, where she studied both chemical engineering and African and African American studies.

Various milestone events and career accomplishments began to fall into (17) place. Jemison was drawn to the astronaut training program, but she (18) realized that she needed more options. To strengthen her credentials, she (19) earned a degree in medicine from Cornell University and worked as a doctor, first in Los Angeles and then with the Peace Corps, in Liberia and Sierra Leone. Since her historic 1992 flight aboard the space shuttle (20) *Endeavour,* she has taught at Dartmouth College, promoted science education, and operated her own science and technology consulting firm.

Yannuzzi believes that for Jemison, "The future is still wide open as (21) she continues to follow her dreams." Raised in a supportive family and (22) determined to reach her goals, Jemison has fashioned a life of challenging and rewarding events and service.

1 Which of the following should Charlene add to her introduction?

  A   the author's name
  B   the editor
  C   the publisher
  D   the book's copyright date

2 Which phrase, if added to the end of sentence 1, would BEST clarify Charlene's thesis statement?

  A   in the space program
  B   in the United States
  C   in economics
  D   in several different fields

for **COLLECTION 3** continued

ANALYZING NONFICTION

3 What paragraph, if any, should Charlene move in order to improve the logical order of her analysis?

A 1
B 2
C 3
D Leave as is.

4 How should sentence 9 be written to create a parallel sentence?

A At home she was allowed the freedom to pursue her interesting thoughts for herself.
B At home she was allowed the freedom of pursuing her natural interests and to think for herself.
C At home she was allowed the freedom to pursue her natural interests and to think for herself.
D Leave as is.

5 Which of the following would make the BEST statement about the element of biography discussed in paragraph 3?

A Jemison had enjoyed college, but now she was eager to begin her career.
B After college, Jemison had to decide what she wanted to do with her future.
C Jemison's character is another element that Yannuzzi explores in this biography.
D Certain character traits were important factors in Jemison's success.

6 Which of the following quotations, if added after sentence 13, would BEST provide evidence for the element of biography discussed in paragraph 3?

A "She was a good student," Yannuzzi explains, "and loved to read."
B "From an early age," Yannuzzi explains, "Mae expressed an interest in science and the mysteries of space."
C By the time she was in high school, Yannuzzi explains, she was "creating opportunities for herself."
D As Yannuzzi explains, "The idea that someday she would fly into space was always in her mind."

7 Which of the following sentences would BEST provide elaboration for the evidence in sentence 16?

A Studying these subjects made her years at Stanford ones she would always remember.
B Studying these subjects showed her determination to gain knowledge of diverse fields.
C Many other people at Stanford also studied these subjects, but Yannuzzi doesn't mention them.
D Jemison's parents must have been very proud of her, since they valued education highly.

GO ON

12 Holt Assessment: Writing, Listening, and Speaking

for COLLECTION 3 *continued*

ANALYZING NONFICTION

8 Which of the following sentences would BEST provide elaboration for the evidence in sentence 21?

A The author suggests that she knows just what the future will hold for Jemison.

B The author suggests that every young person should think about becoming an astronaut.

C The author suggests that Jemison will continue to explore new challenges in the years to come.

D The author suggests that Jemison will continue to be content with her life just the way it is.

9 Charlene's analysis discusses these elements of the biography: setting, character, events. Which needs to be added to the conclusion?

A character
B events
C setting
D Leave as is.

10 Which of the following sentences would be the BEST restatement of Charlene's thesis?

A *Mae Jemison: A Space Biography* shows Jemison as someone whose accomplishments go well beyond her role as an astronaut.

B In *Mae Jemison: A Space Biography*, Yannuzzi portrays Jemison as an ambitious woman whose quest for fame led to her success.

C *Mae Jemison: A Space Biography* is an excellent biography about the first African American woman to become an astronaut.

D Every young person who is searching for a role model should read *Mae Jemison: A Space Biography* by Della A. Yannuzzi.

Writing Workshop: Comparing Media Coverage

DIRECTIONS Read this student essay. Then, read each question that follows the essay. Decide which is the best answer to each question. Mark the letter for that answer.

TV and the Internet – Comparing Apples and Oranges?

Many teens enjoy eating healthful fruits and vegetables on a daily basis.
(1)
However, when one apple is the only meal of the day, it may be a sign of
(2)
a serious health problem — an eating disorder. According to a recent
(3)
television news report on the subject, some teens have taken up a daily
diet that may consist only of a single apple. Since this issue affects many
(4)
in my age group, I looked for more information on the Internet and chose
the most informative source I could find. The television coverage and
(5)
the Internet source contained some similarities but also some striking
differences. Overall, the television coverage was shorter and focused on
(6)
emotional impact, while the online story was more detailed.

The two media features contained valuable information. Both reported
(7)   (8)
on the intense pressure young people face today to be thin. This pressure
(9)
comes from other teens, media coverage, and pop star idols. Both featured
(10)
testimonials from victims of eating disorders and informed audiences of
psychological and physical factors of the disease. Finally, both stories
(11)
provided a list of warning signs and gave suggestions on what to do if
you suspect an eating disorder.

The coverage by the two media was vastly different. The television
(12)   (13)
segment was less than two minutes long, while the online coverage could
take hours to explore. The television coverage provided dramatic footage
(14)
of hauntingly thin teens who obviously were in pain emotionally and
physically. The reporter focused on one particular teen and provided
(15)
insights from her family and her medical advisors. In contrast, the online
(16)
story was less dramatic, but it provided a much wider range of informa-

GO ON

14 Holt Assessment: Writing, Listening, and Speaking

for COLLECTION 4 *continued* **COMPARING MEDIA COVERAGE**

tion. It did not focus on one person but covered many different cases. (17) It included different kinds of eating disorders and their causes. (18) While the television story dealt only with the problem, the online story (19) went on to provide help with solving it. Additionally, (20) the site provided links to related articles, nutrition and medical experts, and treatment facilities. It provided a much more hopeful viewpoint. (21) The television story (22) did not refer viewers to other sources of information or even to a help line.

(23) I preferred the Internet story. The television coverage was affected by (24) time limitations and by a greater need to use drama and emotional impact to attract an audience. Television stories can stir interest about important (25) topics affecting our culture today, but for more information, an interested person may want to consider visiting a reliable online news source.

1 Which sentence should replace sentence 1 as the MOST engaging opening for the essay?

A Many people disregard the most important principles of a good diet.

B Can an apple a day keep the doctor away?

C A well-balanced and nutritional diet is necessary in order to think and function properly.

D Eating disorders have been covered recently in different types of media.

2 Which phrase, if added to the end of sentence 6, would BEST clarify the thesis statement?

A and did not depend on medical information

B and did not report real cases

C and provided many facts and references

D and took little time to understand

for **COLLECTION 4** continued

COMPARING MEDIA COVERAGE

3 Which of the following would BEST state the main point for paragraph 2?

A Internet coverage is more difficult to understand.

B The television coverage relied on reporters who spoke to the audience.

C The television report provided information faster than the Internet report.

D Some similarities in the television and Internet stories were apparent.

4 What transitional word would be BEST to add to the end of sentence 12?

A consequently

B obviously

C however

D in comparison

5 What sentence, if any, should be added after sentence 18 to provide support?

A It interested my entire family and many of my friends.

B It also featured a sports celebrity, who is an admired role model for many teens.

C It also discussed self-esteem issues that can lead to these disorders.

D No support should be added.

6 What supporting information would be BEST to add after sentence 19?

A Some teens never enjoy pizza or hot dogs because of their eating disorders.

B Eating disorders are not contagious.

C It provided specific details about treating anorexia and bulimia.

D The online site was easy to find.

7 Which paragraph, if any, is BEST moved to follow paragraph 4 in order to improve the organization?

A 1

B 2

C 3

D Leave as is.

8 Which of the following sentences would be the BEST reminder of the thesis to replace sentence 23?

A The online story was more complex and less emotional than the television story.

B The television story was a lot more interesting than the Internet story.

C The Internet and television both reach a wide range of people.

D The Internet is here to stay.

9 What should be added as one factor that accounts for differences in the coverage?

A Television coverage deals only with bad news most of the time.

B The online source could be explored at one's own pace.

C More people use the Internet than watch television.

D The Internet is easier to understand.

10 What would be the BEST final idea for readers to consider instead of sentence 25?

A Television news is often sensational, appealing to personal emotions.

B Internet use has become increasingly popular.

C Eating disorders do not affect everyone, but general public awareness is important.

D Leave as is.

16 Holt Assessment: Writing, Listening, and Speaking

Writing Workshop: Persuasive Essay

DIRECTIONS Joe's teacher has assigned the class to write a persuasive essay. Joe believes school overcrowding is an important concern. He wants to send his essay to the local newspaper. Read Joe's essay and answer items 1 through 10.

Planning for Education

Sometimes school enrollment increases sharply, causing overcrowding (1) in classrooms. Ten new housing subdivisions are being built in our area, (2) with fifty houses in each one. If half of the families who move into the (3) houses have two school-age children each, that's an additional five hundred students who will be going to our schools. We all need to think (4) carefully about such a situation.

Several problems arise when there are too many students in a single (5) classroom. Teachers experience more paperwork. Because of the increased (6) (7) numbers of students, teachers must spend a great deal of time preparing materials, grading additional student work, and keeping more records. Additional disciplinary problems develop. The lack of space contributes (8) to more inappropriate behavior and negative consequences.

In addition, students need individual attention. Mr. Blakely says, "It is (9) (10) especially difficult to give individual attention where it is needed. Most (11) of a teacher's time is taken up by making sure the kids get just the basic instruction."

Some people might say that building schools before there are enough (12) students to fill the classrooms is illogical, and they would have a good point.

Traffic and safety concerns are another important reason to avoid over- (13) crowded schools. Students are more vulnerable to traffic accidents if school (14) streets are packed with increased traffic. Halls and locker areas in which (15) students have to jostle their way to class are potentially dangerous environ-

> ments. Almost every week someone trips on the crowded stairs and twists
> (16)
> an ankle or actually falls.
>
> The importance of planning in our own town is <u>out of this world</u>. Every
> (17)   (18)
> parent, teacher, and student should be concerned about the safety of the stu-
> dents in our school district. If the subdivisions are built before new schools
> (19)
> are built, the problems arising from overcrowding will escalate. Quality edu-
> (20)
> cation must be the top priority for this school district.

1 How can the writer BEST improve the beginning of the essay?

- A add statistical evidence
- B add an expert opinion
- C add an emotional appeal
- D add an attention-getting statement

2 The writer can improve the introduction by adding —

- A a sensory detail
- B a clear opinion statement
- C an analogy
- D a piece of evidence

3 What phrase would BEST clarify the type of evidence in sentence 7?

- A To make a comparison,
- B Speaking logically,
- C For example,
- D On the other hand,

4 What should be added to the expert opinion in paragraph 3?

- A more of the quotation from Mr. Blakely
- B an opposing opinion from an expert
- C an explanation of who Mr. Blakely is
- D additional background information

5 What else does the writer need to add to paragraph 3?

- A a transition
- B an emotional appeal
- C another quotation
- D another piece of evidence

6 After sentence 12, the writer should do which of the following?

- A explain case studies
- B name the people mentioned
- C address the counterclaim
- D add facts or statistics

for **COLLECTION 5** *continued* **PERSUASIVE ESSAY**

7 What is the BEST replacement for the phrase out of this world in sentence 17?

A critical
B unreal
C top-notch
D off the charts

8 Where should sentence 18 be moved?

A to paragraph 2
B to paragraph 3
C to paragraph 4
D to paragraph 5

9 Which of the following elements is BEST added to the conclusion?

A additional reasons for the opinion
B a call to action or a summary of reasons
C a clear opinion statement or a counterclaim
D an emotional appeal or a logical appeal

10 Which restatement of opinion should be added to the conclusion?

A Crowded classrooms represent new development and community progress.
B City council members are usually well aware of population changes, but education needs are difficult to predict.
C The problem of school construction needs should be considered before more students are added to already crowded schools.
D Students look to family members to have individual needs met.

Writing Workshop: Describing a Place

for **COLLECTION 6** page 456

DIRECTIONS Read the essay. Then, read each question that follows the essay. Choose the best answer. Then, mark the space for the answer you have chosen.

Perfect for Me

Almost everybody who has ever been in my room hates it. My friends cannot believe how I manage to pack so much stuff into such a small space, and my parents can't stand the clutter.

As I walk through the doorway, the first thing I see is a low, rectangular shape against the window facing me. That's my bed, but you might not know it because it's covered with all my personal stuff.

Lancelot, my golden retriever, is an essential part of my room. He spends a lot of time sprawled out on my bed. When I enter my room, Lancelot jumps down with a clumsy thud and then barks a greeting as he runs to lick my hand with his big pink tongue. It's disgusting. If Lancelot has eaten recently, his breath smells like a nightmare version of fast food.

On my left, I see my wooden dresser, which has a huge chip in the right front leg. On top of the dresser is my CD player. That's where my friend Bobby kicked it by accident while he and I were practicing soccer moves one day. If I squint, the shape of the chip looks like a smiling goalie.

I always listen to classical music in my room because that's what I like to play. When the kettledrums rumble, I feel as if the percussionist were playing me. Books, pens, and paper are laid out in neat piles next to my new computer.

Also on top of my dresser are a lot of fresh apples, oranges, and bananas in a large bowl. When I'm hungry, I just reach for one of my favorite fruits.

On my right, I see my desk. It's orderly, unlike the rest of the room and me! Looking at the tidy arrangement, I feel in control of my life. My desk is a tiny, miniature futuristic city where the buildings are made out of school supplies.

Everything in my room is just the way I like it. If you cannot stand the sight of dirty socks on the floor or the smell of a freshly peeled banana, then my room is no place for you.

GO ON

20 Holt Assessment: Writing, Listening, and Speaking

for **COLLECTION 6** continued

DESCRIBING A PLACE

1. Which of these sentences, if inserted at the end of paragraph 1, would BEST state the controlling impression of the essay?

A Let me show you the place, and you can make your mind up for yourself.

B To me, it's perfect though, full of the things I like, arranged the way I like them.

C Everyone understands how much this place means to me and how important the things in it are.

D Both my friends and my parents are always telling me to clean up my room or else.

2. Which phrase should be added to the end of the second sentence in paragraph 2 to provide factual details?

A —lots of things from school and my house that I often use

B —clothes, sports equipment, books, magazines, and CDs

C —items my parents have asked me to throw away

D —junk I've collected over many months and can't seem to organize

3. Which paragraph contains a description that does not support the controlling impression?

A 2
B 3
C 5
D 6

4. On top of the dresser is my CD player.

To better organize the paper, this sentence in paragraph 4 should be moved to the beginning of—

A paragraph 3
B paragraph 5
C paragraph 6
D paragraph 7

5. When the kettledrums rumble, I feel as if the percussionist were playing me.

Which revision of this sentence adds a sensory detail?

A When the kettledrums rumble, I feel vibration in my stomach, as if the percussionist were right in the room with me.

B When the kettledrums rumble, I feel like a human instrument, as if the percussionist were playing me.

C When the kettledrums rumble, I feel the excitement of the instrument, as if the percussionist were right in the room with me.

D When the kettledrums rumble, I feel like booming along, as if I were the percussionist.

6. Books, pens, and paper are laid out in neat piles next to my new computer.

To better organize the essay, this sentence in paragraph 5 should be moved to paragraph—

A 2
B 3
C 4
D 7

Writing Workshop Tests **21**

7 My desk is a tiny, miniature futuristic city where the buildings are made out of school supplies.

Which word should be deleted from this sentence?

A futuristic
B the
C tiny
D school

8 Which sentence should be inserted at the end of paragraph 6 to show the writer's thoughts and feelings?

A My dad always says that nothing beats a piece of fruit when you're hungry.
B I know that fresh fruit should be an important part of everyone's diet, so I have some every day.
C One of the advantages of the fruit is that it adds a touch of bright color to my drab dresser.
D Somehow, having appetizing food there makes my room seem like the place that has everything I need.

9 If added after the first sentence in the conclusion, which of these would BEST restate the controlling impression and add coherence?

A However, I think a lot of people would like its style.
B It's not orderly, but it's my own retreat.
C I hope to accumulate more furniture.
D Next month I'll straighten it up.

10 Which sentence should be added after the last sentence to BEST wrap up the writer's thoughts and feelings?

A My parents hope I'll grow tired of it someday.
B Why would I want to change anything?
C To my senses, however, my room is trendy.
D However, it's perfect for Lancelot and me.

Writing Workshop: Analyzing a Poem

DIRECTIONS Rosa is writing an analysis of a poem. For her essay, she has chosen the poem "Combing" by Gladys Cardiff. Read Rosa's draft and answer questions 1 through 10.

Imagery and Figurative Language in "Combing"

What connects the different generations of a family? In the poem (1) "Combing," the poet effectively uses the literary elements of imagery (2) and figurative language to show that even everyday activities can create enduring bonds.

The images the poet creates help the reader make connections in (3) the lives of different generations of one family. The poem begins with "Bending, I bow my head" (line 1). The image of a bowed head is repeated, (4) in the "downcast" faces of the speaker's young daughter and great- (5) grandmother (lines 8 and 22). One meaning of *downcast* is "sad." The poet seems to be using the word in its other sense, "turned downward," because (6)   (7) the poem's characters are portrayed as leaning forward with tilted heads.

The color orange is an important visual image. The speaker sees the (8)   (9) orange of her daughter's hair in coils of the stove and in rags torn for rugs. A warm, radiant color, orange suggests the warmhearted affection people (10) feel in the presence of their loved ones.

The speaker also links the generations through images of touch and (11) smell. In line 7, the speaker describes her daughter's hair as "Wet and (12) fragrant"; in line 14, she remembers her own hair, which was freshly washed and "Vinegar-rinsed."

In addition, by using figurative language like metaphors, Cardiff reveals (13) likenesses between seemingly unlike things. One surprising comparison (14) emphasizes that the girl's hair is brightly colored, fresh, and fragrant.

Another metaphor appears in lines 16–17: "The orange coils tick / The (15)

GO ON

Writing Workshop Tests **23**

early hour before school." The sound of the heated coils is compared to the (16) sound of a ticking clock, underscoring the passing of time as generation follows generation. Finally, "Preparing hair" (line 27) is equated with (17) "Plaiting the generations" (line 29). This "simple act" (line 26), the poet (18) suggests, unites different generations just as braiding unites separate strands of hair.

In lines 12–13 the speaker feels her braids "drawn up tight / As a piano (19) wire and singing." Here the speaker imaginatively relives her own child- (20) hood experience. The comparison helps the reader imagine the speaker's (21) precisely arranged hair. It also suggests that the experience lingers in her (22) memory the way a musical note may linger in the air.

Cardiff shows that even the ordinary activities of daily life connect one (23) generation to the next. Vivid images help the reader experience different (24) generations separated by time but linked by everyday activities.

1 What, if placed after sentence 1, would BEST relate the poem to experiences people have in common?

A   Is it achieving vast wealth?
B   Is it exotic travel to foreign lands?
C   Is it famous ancestors?
D   Is it special occasions like birthdays and holidays?

2 What should Rosa add to her introduction?

A   the author's name
B   the setting of the poem
C   her source for the poem
D   her reason for choosing the poem

for **COLLECTION 7** *continued*

ANALYZING A POEM

3 Which phrase, if added to the end of sentence 2, would BEST clarify the thesis statement?

- A between the speaker and her daughter
- B between common experiences
- C between the generations
- D between special occasions

4 Which sentence should Rosa add after sentence 6 to explain how the poet uses the word *downcast*?

- A *Downcast* means "dejected," too.
- B When people are sad, they don't bow their heads.
- C "*Downcast* faces" does not refer to the speaker's family members.
- D However, there is no hint of sadness in the poem.

5 What is the BEST elaboration for the references in sentence 12?

- A These two images emphasize that hair should be wet when it is braided.
- B These two images confirm that hair should smell good after it is washed.
- C These two images emphasize the similarity between the mother's and daughter's experiences.
- D These two images stress the lack of communication between mother and daughter.

6 What, if added after sentence 14, would BEST provide an example for the key literary element discussed in paragraph 5?

- A In lines 5–6, the speaker remarks, "My daughter's hair / Curls against the comb."
- B In lines 7–8, the speaker sees her daughter's hair as "orange / Parings," or peelings.
- C In line 9, the speaker describes her daughter's face as "quiet."
- D In lines 21–22, the speaker relates that "Mathilda rocked her oak-wood / Chair."

7 Which of the following would BEST introduce the key literary element discussed in paragraph 6?

- A Cardiff also uses another type of figurative language, a simile, to convey her message.
- B By using a simile, Cardiff reveals how literary elements can be used to unite the generations.
- C The images that Cardiff uses also make her poem a good one to analyze for an English class.
- D The diction that Cardiff uses also shows that she is a talented poet with original ideas.

8 Which would be the BEST restatement of the thesis to add to the beginning of sentence 23?

- A Through rhyme and repetition,
- B Through references and elaboration,
- C Through her attitude toward the subject,
- D Through imagery and figurative language,

for **COLLECTION 7** continued

ANALYZING A POEM

9 Which would be the BEST addition to the summary of main points?

A Sound devices help the reader hear the speaker's voice in his or her own mind.

B Metaphors and similes help the reader perceive ordinary things in new ways.

C Tone helps the reader perceive the poet's attitude toward her subject.

D Characters help the reader understand the poet's family history.

10 What, if added in the conclusion, would BEST relate the poem to broader themes in life?

A Like the speaker in "Combing," my mother remembers having her hair combed by her own mother.

B "Combing" would be an excellent poem to include in a poetry anthology.

C "Combing" helps us realize that special occasions like birthday parties and family reunions are fun.

D "Combing" helps us realize that each new generation is a link in an ongoing chain.

Writing Workshop: Analyzing a Short Story

DIRECTIONS For his English class, Kevin is writing an analysis of a short story. The story he is analyzing is "The Pedestrian," by Ray Bradbury. Here is Kevin's draft, which may contain problems in style, content, and organization. Read the analysis and answer questions 1 through 10.

A Walk into the Future

In the short story "The Pedestrian,"(1) the author emphasizes the literary elements of point of view, mood, and diction to create a frightening theme about the possible effects of depending too much on technology.

Bradbury uses the limited third-person point of view to emphasize how(2) isolated his character, Leonard Mead, is from the rest of society. With this(3) limited point of view, most aspects of the story are filtered through Mead's thoughts and feelings. The word *pedestrian* can mean "someone who trav-(4) els on foot," as Mead does on his nightly walks, or it can mean "ordinary." Other people's conversations are described only as "whisperings and(5) murmurs." Passing one house, Mead wonders whether he hears a(6) "murmur of laughter." The reader, like Mead, remains unsure; the narra-(7) tor's limited point of view cannot provide an answer.

Through vivid, mood-filled passages, the reader feels Mead's sense of(8) the "buckling concrete walk" underfoot. The reader hears the "silence" of(9) the deserted streets, and breathes the "good crystal frost in the air," all details that enhance a feeling of stark isolation in this vision of the future. Roaming the empty streets is the threatening police car.(10)

Bradbury's skillful choice of words, or diction, helps develop the(11) theme of an eerie society whose citizens have been lulled into apathy by technology. Even the story's title contributes to the theme. Bradbury seems(12)(13) to be using the word in both senses. Comparing Mead's walk with a walk(14) through a "graveyard," the author describes the flickers of light from the screens as "gray phantoms" within "tomb like" buildings. These(15)

for COLLECTION 8 *continued*   **ANALYZING A SHORT STORY**

> comparisons suggest that Mead, on what the reader assumes should be an ordinary walk, is the only one in the city who is fully alive. Only Mead ventures out into the real world; everyone else huddles inside, held ⁽¹⁶⁾ by the hypnotic effects of the images on "viewing screens." Retreating into ⁽¹⁷⁾ make-believe, people have allowed machines to influence their behavior. Civilization now depends completely on technology.
> ⁽¹⁸⁾
>   By using the limited third-person point of view, Bradbury underscores ⁽¹⁹⁾ Leonard Mead's isolation and reinforces the theme. The story's eerie mood ⁽²⁰⁾ also supports a theme of too much technology and its terrible results.

1. Which question, if placed before sentence 1, would MOST grab the readers' attention?

   A If television had not been invented, would more people take long walks at night?

   B What if authorities could confine you to a mental hospital just for taking a walk?

   C Is the future bright for those who like and use technology?

   D Do you know someone who is looking for people and activity?

2. Which of the following should Kevin add to the introduction?

   A the source of the story

   B the date of publication

   C the publisher's name

   D the author's name

3. Which of the following sentences, if added after sentence 1, would BEST clarify the thesis?

   A The story demonstrates that technology, if allowed to rule our lives, may lead to additional freedoms.

   B The story demonstrates that technology in the future will be very different from the way it is today.

   C The story demonstrates that technology, if allowed to rule our lives, may lead to the loss of individual freedoms.

   D The story demonstrates that technology can be very expensive for both taxpayers and the government.

4. Which of the following sentences should be moved to paragraph 4?

   A sentence 2

   B sentence 3

   C sentence 4

   D sentence 5

GO ON

28 Holt Assessment: Writing, Listening, and Speaking

for **COLLECTION 8** continued

ANALYZING A SHORT STORY

5 Which of the following phrases would BEST elaborate on sentence 10?

A under rows of street lights
B the only one Leonard sees that night
C a cold, impersonal automaton
D patrolling the vacant area

6 Which of the following, if placed after sentence 11, would BEST elaborate on Bradbury's use of the word *pedestrian*?

A In Bradbury's imagined future, Leonard Mead is a pedestrian.
B In Bradbury's imagined future, people who control technology are typical.
C In Bradbury's imagined future, Leonard Mead considers watching television an ordinary activity.
D In Bradbury's imagined future, an ordinary act, such as traveling on foot, is considered abnormal.

7 Which of the following modifiers, if substituted for <u>held</u> in sentence 16, would most precisely describe the television viewers?

A stuck
B caught
C restrained
D transfixed

8 In the conclusion, which of the following sentences would BEST restate Kevin's thesis?

A In "The Pedestrian," the author alerts us to the advantages and dangers of a world controlled by technology.
B In "The Pedestrian," point of view, mood, and diction create a moving theme of future technological benefits.
C In "The Pedestrian," point of view, mood, and diction contribute to the theme of the dangers of letting technology govern our lives.
D In "The Pedestrian," point of view, mood, and diction reveal the dangers of walking alone at night.

9 Which key point should be added to the summary in the conclusion?

A diction
B theme
C mood
D Leave as is.

10 Which final comment would BEST connect the analysis to real life?

A Bradbury's story helps us recognize how much technology will improve our lives in the future.
B Bradbury's story helps us recognize that people would rather make their own effort to learn technology.
C Bradbury's story helps us recognize how much of our own lives we have surrendered to technology.
D Bradbury's story helps us recognize that people will appreciate technology even more in the future.

Writing Workshop Tests **29**

NAME _____ CLASS _____ DATE _____

for **COLLECTION 9** *page 706*

Writing Workshop: Research Paper

DIRECTIONS Gail is writing a research paper about the Seneca Falls Convention of 1848. Her research question is *What has been the long-term impact of the Seneca Falls Convention on women's rights?* Read the draft of her paper and answer questions 1 through 15.

The Seneca Falls Convention of 1848:
American Women Join the Civil Rights Movement

In the summer of 1848, around two hundred women and men met in
(1)
Seneca Falls, New York, for the country's first national women's rights convention (Levine 277). Many people preferred to watch the waterfall
(2)
instead of the debates at the Seneca Falls Convention. Women's suffrage,
(3)
or the right to vote, was the focus of debate at the convention. However,
(4)
the participants also drafted demands for other rights, such as property rights and equal education opportunities (Stansell 139). The Seneca Falls
(5)
Convention was very important.

    The planning began with a coincidence and took eight years to
(6)
complete. Elizabeth Cady Stanton and Lucretia Mott met at an anti-
(7)
slavery meeting in London. Stanton was a young newlywed at the time,
(8)
but she was already known to speak her mind on issues of human rights. Mott was a middle-aged Quaker preacher. Stanton and Mott were both
(9)   (10)
upset because women attending the anti-slavery meeting had to sit behind curtains and were not allowed to speak. They were very bored behind
(11)
the curtains. Their shared outrage at not being allowed to participate
(12)
strengthened their desire to fight for women's rights, and they agreed to hold a nationwide meeting to discuss women's rights when they returned home. Eight years later, Stanton, Mott, and others held the convention in
(13)
Stanton's hometown of Seneca Falls (Stansell 134–136).

    The organizers of the Seneca Falls Convention were inspired by the
(14)
anti-slavery movement and by the women's rights movement in Europe

GO ON

30   Holt Assessment: Writing, Listening, and Speaking

(Stansell 133). They probably reasoned that, just as African American men should be given the full rights of United States citizenship, so too should women of all races. Many of the Seneca Falls organizers were already activists in the abolition movement, which fought for the freedom and rights of African Americans. Margaret Fuller noted a similarity in the situations of the two groups, saying, "There exists in the world of men, a tone of feeling towards women as towards slaves."

   A long list of rights were denied to women, stimulating the activists' resentment of their second-class status. Women of the mid-1800s were not allowed to vote, and married women could not own property apart from their husbands. Married women had no legal rights of their own; they were essentially the property of their husbands. In the event of a divorce, women could not claim their own money or their children. Women also were not allowed to attend most universities and therefore could not work in many professions (Osborn). In response to these unfair policies, the convention's participants drafted the Declaration of Sentiments. That statement was modeled after the Declaration of Independence. Its text shows a strong resemblance to the document that inspired it:

>   We hold these truths to be self-evident: that all men and women are created equal; that they are endowed by their Creator with certain inalienable rights; that among these are life, liberty, and the pursuit of happiness. . . .
>
>   Now . . . because women do feel themselves aggrieved, oppressed, and fraudulently deprived of their most sacred rights, we insist that they have immediate admission to all the rights and privileges which belong to them as citizens of the United States. (Stanton)

The Declaration of Sentiments included a list of complaints and a
(26)
matching list of demands for reform. The demand for women's right to
(27)
vote was the most controversial point in the document and was barely
accepted by the convention's participants. There were fears that such a
(28)
demand would be pushing too hard and too fast and would cause others
to laugh off the entire declaration. Some historians believe that the Seneca
(29)
Falls Convention's bold demand for women's suffrage was the main factor
that set off the women's rights movement in the United States (Stansell
141–142). It gave the emerging movement a specific and meaningful goal
(30)
and inspired the ambition to achieve it. The Seneca Falls Convention did
(31)
not bring about significant reforms immediately. Rather, it triggered a
(32)
movement that would bring about gradual change over a period of more
than a hundred years. Those women who attended the Seneca Falls
(33)
Convention started the process of change. Eventually, women gained the
(34)
right to vote as well as all the other rights mentioned in the Declaration
of Sentiments.

Works Cited

Levine, Bruce, et al. Who Built America? Vol. 1. New York: Random House,
  Inc., 1989.

Osborn, Elizabeth R., "The Seneca Falls Convention: Teaching About the
  Rights of Women and the Heritage of the Declaration of Independence."
  ERIC Clearinghouse for Social Studies /Social Science Education, June
  2001. Indiana University. 23 October 2001 <http://www.indiana.edu/
  ~ssdc/senecadig.htm>.

Stansell, Christine. "The Seneca Falls Convention." Eds. James McPherson
  and Alan Brinkley. Days of Destiny: Crossroads in American History.
  New York: Dorling Kindersley Publishing, Inc., 2001, pp. 133–142.

Stanton, Elizabeth C., et al., eds. History of Woman Suffrage. Vol. 1. New
  York, 1881.

NAME _____ CLASS _____ DATE _____

for COLLECTION 9 *continued*

RESEARCH PAPER

1 Which of the following sentences would BEST grab the readers' attention if inserted before sentence 1?

A Seneca Falls, New York, is an interesting town.

B Many people believed that women should not have rights equal to men's.

C In a small town named for a waterfall, women's rights tumbled into place.

D Where did the women's rights movement begin in the United States?

2 Which sentence in the first paragraph should be deleted?

A 1
B 2
C 3
D 4

3 Which of the following sentences would BEST provide background information if inserted after sentence 4?

A These were radical ideas at the time and met with great resistance.

B Men believed that women were not smart enough to attend college.

C The convention participants met in a large church in Seneca Falls.

D Susan B. Anthony did not attend, though many other feminists did.

4 Refer to Gail's research question, stated in the directions, to choose the BEST thesis statement to replace sentence 5.

A The delegates of the Seneca Falls Convention were strong, confident women who were unafraid of being ridiculed.

B The small Seneca Falls Convention set off a movement that would eventually change the face of society and politics in the United States.

C The Seneca Falls Convention turned into a dismal failure, but it did not keep activists from organizing more conventions.

D Leave as is.

5 Which phrase or clause, if added to the beginning of sentence 7, would provide the BEST supporting details?

A Against all odds,

B The idea of a convention devoted to women's rights was born when

C Two educated but shy women,

D Because the abolition movement was closely tied to the women's rights movement,

6 Which sentence should be deleted because it does not support the point of the second paragraph?

A 8
B 9
C 10
D 11

GO ON

Writing Workshop Tests **33**

7 Which sentence should Gail insert before sentence 13 to provide an additional detail that supports the main point of the paragraph?

A Stanton and Mott agreed on most issues, but disagreed on a few important points.

B Stanton had a stern husband who did not approve of her feminist views, while Mott's husband was very supportive.

C Both women developed a dislike of curtains and removed all the draperies from their homes.

D Partly due to poor long-distance communication, they were not able to act immediately on their plans.

8 Which of the following would BEST be inserted after sentence 17?

A proper credit
B an anecdote
C an expert opinion
D another reason

9 Which group of words, if inserted at the beginning of sentence 26, would BEST integrate the long quotation more smoothly into the paper?

A Because convention participants wanted to make men take notice of women,

B Along with this strong statement of equality between men and women,

C Since Elizabeth Stanton wrote the document, she was in a position to demand that

D Even though this was outright plagiarism of the Declaration of Independence,

10 Which one of the following sentences should be added after sentence 28 to support the point made in the fifth paragraph?

A They were right.

B In 1848, half of the adult population were women.

C My neighbor Mr. Smith said that he might have thought the declaration was ridiculous if he had been alive back then (Smith).

D In fact, many people did laugh at the declaration, calling it silly.

11 Choose the BEST revision for the beginning of sentence 28.

A Fears were held that such a demand
B There were many who feared that such a demand
C Many feared that such a demand
D Such a demand would be feared to be

12 Choose the BEST revision for the beginning of sentence 29.

A There exist historians who believe
B I know of some historians who believe
C Historians, who believe
D Leave as is.

13 Where is the BEST place to insert a paragraph break?

A before sentence 27
B before sentence 30
C before sentence 31
D before sentence 32

for COLLECTION 9 *continued*

RESEARCH PAPER

14 Which sentence represents the BEST point to ponder regarding the effects of the convention?

A Did Seneca Falls participants want to gain complete power and political dominance for generations to come?

B Would women today enjoy the rights they do if the Seneca Falls Convention had never occurred?

C Seneca Falls participants accomplished all their goals quickly and effortlessly, despite opposition.

D Since many people expected the women's rights movement to fail, Stanton and Mott were not realistic in their ambitions.

15 Which of the following sentences would be the BEST closing thought to give the readers?

A Women's opportunities continue to improve through the process of protest and reform begun in Seneca Falls, New York, over 150 years ago.

B Most United States women, however, still struggle for their basic rights, which are denied them at every opportunity.

C The early women's rights movement was great because now I can vote and own property.

D Now the women's rights movement is over, and the events of the Seneca Falls convention are not so important anymore.

Writing: Persuading with Cause and Effect

DIRECTIONS Sabrina wrote an essay for her local newspaper. It may contain errors in development and organization. Read the essay and answer questions 1 through 10.

School Starts Too Early

Alice wakes up when her alarm clock rings.(1) She rolls out of bed at 6:00 A.M., takes a hurried shower, gulps breakfast,(2) and starts her hectic day. She will arrive at school by 7:00 for early-morning band practice, attend classes(3) from 7:45 until 3:00, play in a tennis match from 3:45 until 5:30, eat a quick dinner from 6:00 until 6:20, do homework and phone friends until 10:30, and watch a few minutes of television before she falls into bed at 11:00. When the whole process begins again the next morning, she will feel exhausted.(4) The seven hours of sleep she logs is more than many students get,(5) but it is not enough. All across America, sleepy students suffer because(6) school starts so early. Teens need more sleep, and they also learn better later in the day.(7) The time at which school begins is not the best.(8)

Alice is like most other students who have busy schedules.(9) Some work(10) at part-time jobs. Many participate in sports and other school activities.(11) Students like Alice typically spread themselves too thin.(12) Some students(13) need to work, and many are concerned about doing well academically and participating in many activities so that they can get into good colleges.

In some families students must also help with housework and child care.(14) Many families have two working parents, putting even more pressure on(15) teenagers. In order to do well in school, be active, and fulfill their responsi-(16)bilities, they sacrifice sleep time. Few realize what a serious problem this is.(17)

Lack of sleep results in health problems, memory loss, grouchiness, poor(18) concentration, and sleeping in class. Teens average about seven hours(19) of sleep, but research conducted by the National Sleep Foundation has concluded that most adolescents need over nine hours of sleep.

GO ON

36 Holt Assessment: Writing, Listening, and Speaking

for COLLECTION 10 continued

PERSUADING WITH CAUSE AND EFFECT

> Besides problems due to lack of sleep, problems occur because teens' (20) natural sleep rhythms are out of line with school schedules. According to (21) some studies teens suffer not only from lack of sleep but also from sleeping at what seem to be the wrong hours. Schools that have experimented with (22) later starting times report better attendance, improved learning, and a positive reception from teachers and principals.
>
> Because of the problems resulting from teens' sleep habits, I propose a (23) new course of action. Bus schedules will have to change. After-school jobs (24) (25) and activities will need to be rescheduled. Other school staff, such as (26) cafeteria workers, will have to adjust. All of this is true, but the benefits are (27) well worth the effort. If school started later, increased learning, improved (28) morale, and health benefits would far outweigh the inconveniences.

1 Which is the BEST way to rewrite sentence 1 to create an interesting anecdote?

A Alice's alarm clock wakes her up every morning.

B The shrill ring of the alarm startles Alice from a deep sleep.

C Alice sleeps comfortably until her alarm clock wakes her.

D The ring of the alarm clock is loud, and it is what wakes Alice.

2 Which sentence would be the BEST supporting evidence to add after sentence 7?

A Elementary schools often begin even earlier than high schools.

B Research shows that teens are much more alert and better able to concentrate and learn in the afternoon.

C In other countries, school schedules are often very different from those in the United States.

D However, not all schools start at exactly the same time.

3 Which is the BEST way to rewrite sentence 8 to make the opinion statement clearer?

A School begins at a bad time.

B The starting time for school should be changed by an hour.

C School starts too early; it should begin at least one hour later.

D School begins at an hour that students don't like.

4 Which sentence could BEST be added after sentence 12 for an emotional appeal?

A Yet, participation in sports is helpful in developing leadership qualities.

B However, teens enjoy the spending money they acquire from jobs.

C The sleepy student who is struggling and overworked could be in your family.

D Many adults remember how busy they were in high school.

GO ON

Writing Workshop Tests **37**

5 Which sentence, if added after sentence 13, would provide the BEST supporting evidence?

A Baby-sitting is a favorite part-time job of many teens.

B High school students spend too many hours studying for challenging classes.

C Honors classes do not allow time for extracurricular activities.

D In fact, colleges typically prefer to admit well-rounded students.

6 Which is the BEST evidence to add after sentence 21?

A Several studies have been conducted to see if students fell asleep in class.

B Teachers will tell you that they have seen students fall asleep in class.

C One study found that 20 percent of students fall asleep in class.

D It is obvious that students cannot learn if they fall asleep in class.

7 What sentence, if added after sentence 23, would be the BEST call to action?

A Please do something about the problem of sleepy students.

B Please write your school board members about establishing a later start time.

C Please consider all the arguments presented in this essay.

D Please get involved with the issue of school start time.

8 If inserted before sentence 24, which sentence would BEST address possible counterclaims?

A Many school workers would appreciate a later start time.

B Most school administrators would need to rework the entire class schedule.

C If you ask students, almost all of them will favor a later start.

D Some people think that a later start will cause other problems.

9 Which word or phrase would BEST be added to the beginning of sentence 24?

A As a result,

B But

C On the other hand,

D Especially,

10 Which sentence would provide the strongest concluding statement?

A There are many articles available on this important subject.

B Add this to the list of things that should be considered carefully.

C Join the movement to push the school bell to a later hour.

D Ask your student's teachers for their opinions about school start time.

for **COLLECTION 11** page 1040

Writing Workshop: Comparing a Play and a Film

DIRECTIONS The following is a rough draft of an essay comparing a scene in Shakespeare's play *Henry V* with a scene in Kenneth Branagh's film of the same name. The essay may contain errors in development and organization. Read the essay and answer questions 1 through 10.

Henry V: From Famous Play to Rousing Film

Throughout history, battle cries have stirred the spirits of soldiers.(1) Some of the most famous were written by William Shakespeare: "Once(2) more unto the breach, dear friends, once more" is one.(3) "Cry, 'God for Harry, England, and Saint George!'" is another.(4) These lines come from a(5) famous battle scene in a play by William Shakespeare. A film version of(6) the play was made a number of years ago. It was a triumph. New life was(7)(8) breathed into this timeless classic by Kenneth Branagh, the director and star, who used narrative and film techniques very effectively.

The real power of the play and the movie comes from the speeches(9) Shakespeare wrote for the king and from Branagh's interpretations of those speeches. The basic story of the king is rather simple. When Branagh(10)(11) delivers the line, "Once more unto the breach, dear friends, once more," he is mounted on a white horse. No such stage direction is found in the play,(12) so it was the film director's choice, and a very effective one. As the king,(13) Henry V speaks passionately about pursuing English interests in France. A careful comparison of the play's text to the film reveals that only about(14) six lines from the original play have been deleted for the movie version.

The battle scene includes close-ups of the king, wide-angle shots of the(15) army, and brief close-ups of specific soldiers. The background is a dark(16) night, illuminated by blazing flashes of fire along with the roar of cannons or thunder. This combination of darkness, dramatic flashes of light, and(17) carefully timed explosions enhances the effect of the text. As Henry(18) delivers his stirring and motivational words, the nods, grunts, and facial

GO ON

Writing Workshop Tests   **39**

expressions of the soldiers show that his speech is winning them over. They grin, shout, wave their swords, and charge with enthusiasm.
(19) In the film, each time an important line is delivered by Henry V, his
(20) magnificent horse rears up on its haunches, flames flash in the background, and an explosion punctuates his words. The play's text was dramatic
(21) when Shakespeare wrote it more than four hundred years ago, and Kenneth Branagh's invigorating film interpretation is an inspiring tribute to the original.

1 Which sentences could BEST be added to the beginning of the essay to create a more engaging introduction?

A William Shakespeare is one of the most famous playwrights in English literature. He also wrote poetry.

B Kenneth Branagh is a Shakespearean actor and director. He has appeared in many plays and films.

C Soldiers charge into battle. Their eyes are ablaze, and they scream at the top of their lungs.

D Shakespeare's plays included tragedies, comedies, and histories. *Henry V* is a history play.

2 How can sentence 5 BEST be changed to appropriately identify the play?

A Both of these lines come from *Henry V*, one of Shakespeare's plays.

B These lines come from a play written by William Shakespeare in 1599.

C These lines were written by Shakespeare for a history play.

D These lines come from Act III, Scene I of William Shakespeare's play *Henry V*.

3 How can sentence 6 BEST be changed to provide readers with information about the context of the movie?

A The movie version of *Henry V* came out in 1989.

B Kenneth Branagh has appeared in and directed many movies and plays.

C It was successful because it came out during a war.

D In the movie, not only did Branagh play King Henry, but his then wife played Katharine of France.

4 How should sentence 8 be rewritten using active voice?

A Using modern film techniques to breathe new life into the timeless classic was Kenneth Branagh, the director and star.

B Interest was added by special effects and careful film techniques.

C Kenneth Branagh, the director and star, used techniques of modern film-making to breathe new life into the timeless classic.

D Leave as is.

GO ON

40   Holt Assessment: Writing, Listening, and Speaking

for **COLLECTION 11** *continued*

COMPARING A PLAY AND A FILM

5 Which sentence could BEST be deleted from paragraph 2 because it does least to support the thesis?

A 9
B 10
C 12
D 14

6 Which sentence in paragraph 2 should become the second sentence of the paragraph to better organize the evidence?

A 9
B 11
C 12
D 13

7 Which sentence, if added, would BEST introduce the discussion of film techniques in paragraph 3?

A Dialogue in the film closely follows dialogue in the play.
B The film was released at a time when England was at war.
C Special effects add drama to the play's dialogue.
D The film's director is also its featured actor.

8 Which sentence could BEST be added before sentence 18 to discuss the film techniques described?

A Filming has changed a lot since the days of primitive, hand-held cameras.
B Branagh probably studied filmmaking prior to his successful movie career.
C As King Henry speaks to his troops, the camera deftly cuts back and forth.
D Branagh probably deleted six lines to make the speech more dramatic.

9 What sentence, if added in the last paragraph, would BEST restate the essay's thesis?

A It is difficult to compare a four-hundred-year-old play with a movie made less than twenty years ago.
B Branagh's narrative and film techniques bring extra vitality to the dramatic four-hundred-year-old play.
C William Shakespeare and Kenneth Branagh both have demonstrated a keen interest in history.
D The drama of Henry V as depicted by both Shakespeare and Branagh differs from historical record.

10 Which line could BEST be added as a concluding thought?

A Some scholars believe that William Shakespeare did not write the plays attributed to him.
B Historians do not agree, however, that all of the events in the play are accurate.
C In my opinion, it is easier to make a tragedy lively than to do so for a history.
D In addition, the film version brings the play to a much wider audience.

Writing Workshop Tests

Writing: Business Letter

for COLLECTION 12 — page 1084

DIRECTIONS In history class, Brad learned that one of his favorite vacation spots is historically important. He wrote a letter of inquiry to the government office responsible for managing the area and requested more information. Read Brad's draft and answer questions 1 through 10.

2371 Lone Pine Drive

Casper, WY 82601

February 3, 2003

Director, Long Distance Trails Office

National Park Service

P.O. Box 45155

Salt Lake City, UT 84145

Dear Director:

I want to know about the Wyoming portion of the Oregon Trail that settlers
(1)
took on their way to Oregon. My class studied that trail, and I want to
(2)
know more about Wyoming because that's where I'm from.

   Tell me where the trail comes into Wyoming and where it leaves.
   (3)
Do you have any map, because I want one. My teacher, Mr. Smithers, says
(4)   (5)
pioneers went right through the Wind River Mountains in the Rockies up
north. I aim to prove he's wrong, because I have been there. There's no
       (6)   (7)
way wagons and cows could make it through mountains like those. Mr.
                                                              (8)
Smithers is usually right though.

   If you could give me this stuff, I'd be one happy camper.
   (9)

Brad Meeker
(10)

GO ON →

42 Holt Assessment: Writing, Listening, and Speaking

| NAME | CLASS | DATE |

for **COLLECTION 12** continued

BUSINESS LETTER

1 To maintain a consistent block style, all paragraphs should—

A be the same length
B be indented
C align with the salutation
D name the recipient

2 Which revision to the heading and inside address should Brad make?

A add his name to the top line
B move them to the left margin
C delete his own address
D spell out Wyoming

3 What is the BEST revision of sentence 1 in order to improve the beginning statement?

A mention an important acquaintance by name
B summarize Brad's summer travels
C use a more polite tone to make the request
D indicate how many settlers traveled through Wyoming

4 What general revision should be made to the first paragraph?

A mention the historical significance of the settlers
B add more information about Brad's history class
C delete the reference to where Brad lives
D include more specifics about what is being requested

5 What should the writer do to BEST revise the first two sentences of the second paragraph?

A use more courteous language
B add his hometown as a reference to the trail location
C provide more information about state geography
D request several maps of the state

6 Which is the BEST revision, if any, of sentence 7?

A When I was there, I didn't see any cattle or wagons getting through.
B I have been in that area and cannot believe that wagons and cattle could get through there.
C However, I have hiked in that area and wonder how wagons and cattle could make it through those mountains.
D Leave as is.

7 Sentence 6 needs to be edited because it contains—

A a contraction
B rude words
C too many definitions
D names of places

8 Which sentence, if any, should be added after sentence 9 to provide information the recipient needs to know?

A When can you send me the information I need?
B If possible, I would like the information by the end of February.
C My class will be studying westward expansion for three weeks.
D Leave as is.

GO ON

Writing Workshop Tests **43**

for **COLLECTION 12** continued

BUSINESS LETTER

9 Which sentence, if any, should be deleted because it contains information the recipient does not need to know?

A 5
B 6
C 8
D None should be deleted.

10 Which would be the BEST closing?

A Love
B Good luck
C Have a nice day
D Sincerely

NAME _____ CLASS _____ DATE _____ SCORE _____

Answer Sheet 1
Collection _____

Writing Workshop

1 Ⓐ Ⓑ Ⓒ Ⓓ   5 Ⓐ Ⓑ Ⓒ Ⓓ   8   Ⓐ Ⓑ Ⓒ Ⓓ
2 Ⓐ Ⓑ Ⓒ Ⓓ   6 Ⓐ Ⓑ Ⓒ Ⓓ   9   Ⓐ Ⓑ Ⓒ Ⓓ
3 Ⓐ Ⓑ Ⓒ Ⓓ   7 Ⓐ Ⓑ Ⓒ Ⓓ   10 Ⓐ Ⓑ Ⓒ Ⓓ
4 Ⓐ Ⓑ Ⓒ Ⓓ

NAME _____ CLASS _____ DATE _____ SCORE _____

Answer Sheet 2

Collection _____

Writing Workshop

1 Ⓐ Ⓑ Ⓒ Ⓓ   6 Ⓐ Ⓑ Ⓒ Ⓓ   11 Ⓐ Ⓑ Ⓒ Ⓓ
2 Ⓐ Ⓑ Ⓒ Ⓓ   7 Ⓐ Ⓑ Ⓒ Ⓓ   12 Ⓐ Ⓑ Ⓒ Ⓓ
3 Ⓐ Ⓑ Ⓒ Ⓓ   8 Ⓐ Ⓑ Ⓒ Ⓓ   13 Ⓐ Ⓑ Ⓒ Ⓓ
4 Ⓐ Ⓑ Ⓒ Ⓓ   9 Ⓐ Ⓑ Ⓒ Ⓓ   14 Ⓐ Ⓑ Ⓒ Ⓓ
5 Ⓐ Ⓑ Ⓒ Ⓓ   10 Ⓐ Ⓑ Ⓒ Ⓓ   15 Ⓐ Ⓑ Ⓒ Ⓓ

Answer Key

Collection 1
Autobiographical Narrative

p. 3

1. 4th option (significance of experience)
2. 3rd option (details about places)
3. 2nd option (details about feelings)
4. 3rd option (details about feelings)
5. 3rd option (details about places)
6. 1st option (details about places)
7. 3rd option (lessons learned)
8. 3rd option (sequence of events)
9. 2nd option (precise language)
10. 2nd option (significance of experience)

Collection 2
Short Story

p. 6

1. A (introduction to main character)
2. B (narrative details)
3. D (vivid action verbs)
4. C (sensory details)
5. D (narrative details)
6. B (conflict)
7. C (sensory details)
8. B (rising action)
9. D (climax)
10. C (suggestion of theme)

Collection 3
Analyzing Nonfiction

p. 10

1. A (author)
2. D (thesis statement)
3. D (logical order)
4. C (parallel sentences)
5. D (elements of biography)
6. C (evidence)
7. B (elaboration)
8. C (elaboration)
9. C (summary of elements)
10. A (restatement of thesis)

Collection 4
Comparing Media Coverage

p. 14

1. B (engaging opening)
2. C (clear thesis)
3. D (point of comparison)
4. C (transitional words and phrases)
5. C (support for point of comparison)
6. C (support for point of comparison)
7. D (organization)
8. A (reminder of thesis)
9. B (factors that account for differences)
10. C (final idea to consider)

Collection 5
Persuasive Essay

p. 17

1. D (attention-getting statement)
2. B (opinion statement)
3. C (evidence)
4. C (expert opinion)
5. D (evidence)
6. C (counterclaims)
7. A (overused expressions)
8. D (logical organization)
9. B (call to action)
10. C (opinion restatement)

Writing Workshop Tests

Answer Key (continued)

Collection 6
Describing a Place

p. 20
1. B (controlling impression)
2. B (factual details)
3. D (figurative details)
4. B (spatial order)
5. A (sensory detail)
6. D (organization)
7. C (repetitive adjectives)
8. D (writer's thoughts)
9. B (restatement of controlling impression)
10. D (writer's thoughts and feelings)

Collection 7
Analyzing a Poem

p. 23
1. D (relationship to common experiences)
2. A (author's name in introduction)
3. C (clear thesis statement)
4. D (key literary element)
5. C (elaboration)
6. B (reference for element)
7. A (key literary element)
8. D (reminder of thesis)
9. B (summary of main points)
10. D (relationship to broader themes in life)

Collection 8
Analyzing a Short Story

p. 27
1. B (summary of story)
2. D (author's name)
3. C (thesis with focus element)
4. C (one key point in each paragraph)
5. C (key point elaborated)
6. D (key point elaborated)
7. D (precise description)
8. C (restatement of thesis)
9. A (summary of key points)
10. C (connection to real life)

Collection 9
Research Paper

p. 30
1. C (readers' attention)
2. B (logical order)
3. A (background information)
4. B (thesis statement)
5. B (support of main points)
6. D (logical order)
7. D (support of main points)
8. A (proper credit)
9. B (integrated quotation)
10. D (elaboration)
11. C (There is/There are)
12. D (There is/There are)
13. C (each point in separate paragraph)
14. B (point to ponder)
15. A (closing thought)

Collection 10
Persuading with Cause and Effect

p. 36
1. B (anecdote in introduction)
2. B (supporting evidence)
3. C (clear opinion statement)
4. C (emotional appeal)
5. D (supporting evidence)
6. C (supporting evidence)
7. B (call to action)

Answer Key *(continued)*

8. D (counterclaims)
9. A (clue words)
10. C (final statement)

Collection 11

Comparing a Play and a Film

p. 39

1. C (interesting opening)
2. D (original play and its film version)
3. A (original play and its film version)
4. C (active voice)
5. B (support of discussion)
6. D (point-by-point organization)
7. C (analysis of techniques)
8. C (evidence of film techniques)
9. B (restated thesis)
10. D (question to think about)

Collection 12

Business Letter

p. 42

1. C (proper format)
2. B (proper format)
3. C (courtesy)
4. D (clarity)
5. A (courtesy)
6. C (clarity)
7. A (formal style)
8. B (clarity)
9. C (clarity)
10. D (tone)

Workshop Scales and Rubrics

NAME _____ CLASS _____ DATE _____

for COLLECTION 1 *page 78*

ANALYTICAL SCALE

Writing: Autobiographical Narrative

Use the chart below (and the rubric on pages 54–55) to evaluate an autobiographical narrative. Circle the numbers that best indicate how well the criteria are met. With these ten criteria, the lowest possible score is 0, the highest 40.

4 = Clearly meets this criterion
3 = Makes a serious effort to meet this criterion and is fairly successful
2 = Makes some effort to meet this criterion but with little success
1 = Does not achieve this criterion
0 = Unscorable

CRITERIA FOR EVALUATION	RATINGS
Genre, Organization, and Focus	
Introduction includes an engaging opening.	4 3 2 1
Introduction supplies background information.	4 3 2 1
Introduction hints at the significance of the experience.	4 3 2 1
Body includes plenty of details describing people, places, and events.	4 3 2 1
Order of events is clear.	4 3 2 1
Details about narrator's thoughts and feelings are included.	4 3 2 1
Precise, vivid language shows the scene.	4 3 2 1
Conclusion reflects on what was learned or changed as a result of the experience and reveals its significance.	4 3 2 1
Language Conventions	
Standard English spelling, punctuation, capitalization, and manuscript form are used appropriately for this grade level.	4 3 2 1
Standard English sentence and paragraph structure, grammar, usage, and diction are used appropriately for this grade level.	4 3 2 1
Total Points:	

Workshop Scales and Rubrics

NAME _____ CLASS _____ DATE _____

for **COLLECTION 1** page 78

ANALYTICAL SCORING RUBRIC

Writing: Autobiographical Narrative

CRITERIA FOR EVALUATION	SCORE POINT 4	SCORE POINT 3	SCORE POINT 2	SCORE POINT 1
Genre, Organization, and Focus				
Introduction includes an engaging opening.	An engaging opening grabs the readers' attention.	Introduction takes readers into account but does not grab their attention.	Introduction is only partially successful at addressing readers' interests.	Introduction lacks an engaging opening and fails to interest the reader.
Introduction supplies background information.	Introduction supplies clear information that effectively establishes the background of the narrative.	Introduction supplies some necessary background information.	Introduction hints at or includes only partial background information.	Background information is missing or irrelevant.
Introduction hints at the significance of the experience.	Introduction hints at the significance of the experience and sets up the controlling impression.	Introduction hints at the significance of the experience in a general way.	Introduction gives unrelated significance to experience.	Significance of the experience is not addressed.
Body includes plenty of details describing people, places, and events.	Body includes plenty of details, including concrete sensory details and dialogue, about people, places, and events that create effective images.	Body includes details about people, places, and events, but several details are not concrete or clear.	Body includes few details about people, places, and events, or details are confusing.	Description of people, places, and events is minimal.
Order of events is clear.	Order of events is in clear chronological order with transitional words that suggest changes in time.	Events are related mostly in chronological order.	Some events are related in chronological order, while other events seem out of place.	Events are related in random order.
Details about narrator's thoughts and feelings are included.	Details about narrator's thoughts and feelings are included, sometimes through interior monologue.	Some details about narrator's thoughts and feelings are included.	Narrator's thoughts and feelings must be inferred.	Narrator's thoughts and feelings are missing from narrative.
Precise, vivid language shows the scene.	Precise, vivid descriptive language shows the scene and brings it to life.	Precise language is frequently used but is not vivid enough to completely show the scene.	Precise, vivid language is sparse.	Language is vague and unclear.

WORKSHOP SCALES AND RUBRICS

54 Holt Assessment: Writing, Listening, and Speaking

for COLLECTION 1 *continued*

ANALYTICAL SCORING RUBRIC

CRITERIA FOR EVALUATION	SCORE POINT 4	SCORE POINT 3	SCORE POINT 2	SCORE POINT 1
Conclusion reflects on what was learned or changed as a result of the experience and reveals its significance.	Conclusion reflects on what was specifically learned or changed as a result of the experience and reveals its significance.	Conclusion reflects on what was learned or changed as a result of the experience and reveals its significance in a general way.	In the conclusion, significance of experience seems unrelated to narrative.	Conclusion omits any reference to the significance of the experience.
Language Conventions				
Standard English spelling, punctuation, capitalization, and manuscript form are used appropriately for this grade level.	Standard English spelling, punctuation, capitalization, and manuscript form are used appropriately for this grade level throughout the narrative.	Standard English spelling, punctuation, capitalization, and manuscript form are used appropriately for this grade level, with few problems.	Inconsistent use of standard English spelling, punctuation, capitalization, and manuscript form disrupts readers' comprehension.	Minimal use of standard English spelling, punctuation, capitalization, and manuscript form confuses the readers.
Standard English sentence and paragraph structure, grammar, usage, and diction are used appropriately for this grade level.	Standard English sentence and paragraph structure, grammar, usage, and diction are used appropriately for this grade level throughout the narrative.	Standard English sentence and paragraph structure, grammar, usage, and diction are used appropriately for this grade level, with few problems.	Inconsistent use of standard English sentence and paragraph structure, grammar, usage, and diction disrupts readers' comprehension.	Minimal use of standard English sentence and paragraph structure, grammar, usage, and diction confuses the readers.

WORKSHOP SCALES AND RUBRICS

Workshop Scales and Rubrics

NAME _____ CLASS _____ DATE _____

for **COLLECTION 1** page 86

ANALYTICAL SCALE

Speaking: Oral Narrative

Use the chart below to evaluate an oral narrative. Circle the numbers that best indicate how well the criteria are met. With these eight criteria, the lowest possible score is 0, the highest 32.

4 = Clearly meets this criterion
3 = Makes a serious effort to meet this criterion and is fairly successful
2 = Makes some effort to meet this criterion but with little success
1 = Does not achieve this criterion
0 = Unscorable

CRITERIA FOR EVALUATION	RATINGS
Content, Organization, and Delivery	
The setting locates events in specific places.	4 3 2 1
Vocabulary and sensory details sound natural and vivid enough to create images in listeners' minds.	4 3 2 1
Chronological order and transitional words help listeners follow the events of the experience.	4 3 2 1
The conclusion directly states the significance of the experience.	4 3 2 1
Verbal techniques (pitch, volume, and rate or pace) help show the meaning of the experience.	4 3 2 1
Nonverbal techniques (gestures, eye contact, and facial expressions) add meaning to narrative.	4 3 2 1
Note cards, if used, remind speaker of details.	4 3 2 1
Language Conventions	
Standard English grammar, usage, and diction are used appropriately for this grade level.	4 3 2 1
Total Points:	

WORKSHOP SCALES AND RUBRICS

56   Holt Assessment: Writing, Listening, and Speaking

NAME _____ CLASS _____ DATE _____

for COLLECTION 2 *page 154*

ANALYTICAL SCALE

Writing: Short Story

Use the chart below (and the rubric on pages 58–59) to evaluate a short story. Circle the numbers that best indicate how well the criteria are met. With these ten criteria, the lowest possible score is 0, the highest 40.

4 = Clearly meets this criterion
3 = Makes a serious effort to meet this criterion and is fairly successful
2 = Makes some effort to meet this criterion but with little success
1 = Does not achieve this criterion
0 = Unscorable

CRITERIA FOR EVALUATION	RATINGS
Genre, Organization, and Focus	
Story begins with intriguing event or introduction to main character.	4 3 2 1
Beginning introduces conflict.	4 3 2 1
Beginning establishes setting and narrator's point of view.	4 3 2 1
Narrative and sensory details and dialogue develop the plot, setting, and main character.	4 3 2 1
Action verbs depict action precisely.	4 3 2 1
Rising action of plot is fully developed and organized in chronological order.	4 3 2 1
Climax brings the conflict to a head.	4 3 2 1
The resolution is believable and suggests the theme of the story.	4 3 2 1
Language Conventions	
Standard English spelling, punctuation, capitalization, and manuscript form are used appropriately for this grade level.	4 3 2 1
Standard English sentence and paragraph structure, grammar, usage, and diction are used appropriately for this grade level.	4 3 2 1
Total Points:	

Workshop Scales and Rubrics

NAME _____ CLASS _____ DATE _____

for **COLLECTION 2** page 154

ANALYTICAL SCORING RUBRIC

Writing: Short Story

CRITERIA FOR EVALUATION	SCORE POINT 4	SCORE POINT 3	SCORE POINT 2	SCORE POINT 1
Genre, Organization, and Focus				
Story begins with intriguing event or introduction to main character.	Story begins with intriguing event or engaging introduction to main character.	Story begins with a simple event or introduction to main character.	Story refers to an event or names the main character.	Story's beginning is dull and omits reference to main character.
Beginning introduces conflict.	Beginning clearly introduces external or internal conflict.	Conflict is introduced, but it is not clear.	Conflict is difficult to discern.	Conflict is not apparent.
Beginning establishes setting and narrator's point of view.	Beginning establishes a vivid setting, and first-person or third-person omniscient narrator's point of view is maintained.	Beginning establishes setting, but narrator's point of view is not consistent.	Beginning simply names setting, and narrator's point of view is unclear.	Setting is not described, and narrator's point of view is unknown.
Narrative and sensory details and dialogue develop the plot, setting, and main character.	Plenty of lively narrative and sensory details and dialogue bring the plot, setting, and main character to life.	Narrative and sensory details and dialogue develop the plot, setting, and main character, but story lacks enough specific details.	Few narrative and sensory details and dialogue barely develop the plot, setting, and main character.	Sparse narrative and sensory details and dialogue leave the plot and main character weak and impossible to visualize.
Action verbs depict action precisely.	Precise, vivid action verbs depict action in a lively, entertaining style throughout the story.	Several vivid action verbs depict most action precisely.	Few action verbs are sprinkled among the dull verbs.	Verbs are dull, passive, and/or general.
Rising action of plot is fully developed and organized in chronological order.	Rising action of plot is fully developed and organized in clear chronological order.	Rising action of plot is organized in chronological order, with few diversions.	Chronological order is not maintained and disrupts the rising action.	The action rambles with no logical sequence or rising conflict.
Climax brings the conflict to a head.	Climax brings the conflict to a head with effective emotional impact.	Climax brings the conflict to a head but lacks some emotional impact.	Climax is inappropriately placed, with the story's high point too early in the action.	Climax is missing or inappropriate.

WORKSHOP SCALES AND RUBRICS

58 Holt Assessment: Writing, Listening, and Speaking

NAME _____ CLASS _____ DATE _____

for **COLLECTION 2** *continued* **ANALYTICAL SCORING RUBRIC**

CRITERIA FOR EVALUATION	SCORE POINT 4	SCORE POINT 3	SCORE POINT 2	SCORE POINT 1
The resolution is believable and suggests the theme of the story.	The resolution, with its unwinding events, is believable and clearly suggests the significant theme of the story.	The resolution is believable, but abrupt, and suggests the theme of the story.	The resolution is hard to believe, and it is difficult to discern the theme of the story.	The resolution is unrealistic and unrelated to a possible theme of the story.
Language Conventions				
Standard English spelling, punctuation, capitalization, and manuscript form are used appropriately for this grade level.	Standard English spelling, punctuation, capitalization, and manuscript form are used appropriately for this grade level throughout the story.	Standard English spelling, punctuation, capitalization, and manuscript form are used appropriately for this grade level, with few problems.	Inconsistent use of standard English spelling, punctuation, capitalization, and manuscript form disrupts readers' comprehension.	Minimal use of standard English spelling, punctuation, capitalization, and manuscript form confuses the readers.
Standard English sentence and paragraph structure, grammar, usage, and diction are used appropriately for this grade level.	Standard English sentence and paragraph structure, grammar, usage, and diction are used appropriately for this grade level throughout the story.	Standard English sentence and paragraph structure, grammar, usage, and diction are used appropriately for this grade level, with few problems.	Inconsistent use of standard English sentence and paragraph structure, grammar, usage, and diction disrupts readers' comprehension.	Minimal use of standard English sentence and paragraph structure, grammar, usage, and diction confuses the readers.

WORKSHOP SCALES AND RUBRICS

Workshop Scales and Rubrics

Writing: Analyzing Nonfiction

for COLLECTION 3 *page 232*

ANALYTICAL SCALE

Use the chart below (and the rubric on pages 61–62) to evaluate an analysis of nonfiction. Circle the numbers that best indicate how well the criteria are met. With these eleven criteria, the lowest possible score is 0, the highest 44.

- **4** = Clearly meets this criterion
- **3** = Makes a serious effort to meet this criterion and is fairly successful
- **2** = Makes some effort to meet this criterion but with little success
- **1** = Does not achieve this criterion
- **0** = Unscorable

CRITERIA FOR EVALUATION	RATINGS
Genre, Organization, and Focus	
Introduction contains biography's title and author.	4 3 2 1
Introduction includes background information about biography's subject.	4 3 2 1
Thesis in introduction is clear.	4 3 2 1
Information about elements of biography—character, events, and setting—support thesis.	4 3 2 1
Organizational pattern is easy to follow.	4 3 2 1
All pieces of evidence support the discussion of each element.	4 3 2 1
Elaboration explains evidence.	4 3 2 1
Ideas are expressed in balanced, parallel sentences.	4 3 2 1
Conclusion summarizes the elements of biography and restates the thesis.	4 3 2 1
Language Conventions	
Standard English spelling, punctuation, capitalization, and manuscript form are used appropriately for this grade level.	4 3 2 1
Standard English sentence and paragraph structure, grammar, usage, and diction are used appropriately for this grade level.	4 3 2 1
Total Points:	

WORKSHOP SCALES AND RUBRICS

Holt Assessment: Writing, Listening, and Speaking

for COLLECTION 3 page 232

ANALYTICAL SCORING RUBRIC

Writing: Analyzing Nonfiction

CRITERIA FOR EVALUATION	SCORE POINT 4	SCORE POINT 3	SCORE POINT 2	SCORE POINT 1
Genre, Organization, and Focus				
Introduction contains biography's title and author.	Introduction contains biography's title and author.	Introduction contains biography's title or author.	Biography's title or author appears in the paper, but not in the introduction.	No title or author is mentioned.
Introduction includes background information about biography's subject.	Introduction includes essential background information appropriate to audience about biography's subject.	Introduction includes background information about biography's subject, but information is unimportant or inappropriate for audience.	Introduction includes sparse or irrelevant background information about biography's subject.	Introduction includes no background information.
Thesis in introduction is clear.	Thesis in introduction clearly states biographer's main idea about the subject of the biography.	Thesis in introduction merely names the subject of the biography rather than stating the biographer's main idea.	Thesis in introduction states the subject of the biography in ambiguous terms.	Introduction lacks thesis.
Information about elements of biography—character, events, and setting—support thesis.	Information about elements of biography—character, events, and setting—support thesis and help readers understand the subject.	Most information relates directly to thesis, although some relationships are unclear.	Little information relates directly to thesis, but most is unrelated or it is difficult to discern the relationship to the thesis.	Information is unrelated to thesis.
Organizational pattern is easy to follow.	Organizational pattern is logical order (e.g., order of importance) and is easy to follow.	Organizational pattern is logical order and is relatively easy to follow.	Organizational pattern is confusing.	Organization is random.
All pieces of evidence support the discussion of each element.	All pieces of evidence explain and support the discussion of each element and make clear connections for the reader.	Pieces of evidence support most elements.	A few pieces of evidence support some elements, but other elements lack evidence.	Elements are not supported by evidence, or evidence is unrelated to elements.

Workshop Scales and Rubrics **61**

NAME _____ CLASS _____ DATE _____

for **COLLECTION 3** continued   **ANALYTICAL SCORING RUBRIC**

WORKSHOP SCALES AND RUBRICS

CRITERIA FOR EVALUATION	SCORE POINT 4	SCORE POINT 3	SCORE POINT 2	SCORE POINT 1
Elaboration explains evidence.	Effective and clear elaboration explains evidence.	Elaboration explains most evidence.	Elaboration of evidence is sparse.	Supportive elaboration is missing.
Ideas are expressed in balanced, parallel sentences.	Ideas are appropriately and effectively expressed in balanced, parallel sentences.	Most ideas are expressed in balanced, parallel sentences.	Several sentences are unbalanced or awkward in structure.	Sentences lack parallel structure and are typically unbalanced.
Conclusion summarizes the elements of biography and restates the thesis.	Conclusion succinctly and in a fresh manner summarizes the elements of biography and restates the thesis.	Conclusion summarizes the elements of biography and restates the thesis, but lacks clarity.	Conclusion is ambiguous or misstates the thesis and the elements of biography.	Conclusion either lacks summary of the elements of biography and restatement of thesis, ends abruptly, or rambles.

Language Conventions

Standard English spelling, punctuation, capitalization, and manuscript form are used appropriately for this grade level.	Standard English spelling, punctuation, capitalization, and manuscript form are used appropriately for this grade level throughout the essay.	Standard English spelling, punctuation, capitalization, and manuscript form are used appropriately for this grade level, with few problems.	Inconsistent use of standard English spelling, punctuation, capitalization, and manuscript form disrupts readers' comprehension.	Minimal use of standard English spelling, punctuation, capitalization, and manuscript form confuses the readers.
Standard English sentence and paragraph structure, grammar, usage, and diction are used appropriately for this grade level.	Standard English sentence and paragraph structure, grammar, usage, and diction are used appropriately for this grade level throughout the essay.	Standard English sentence and paragraph structure, grammar, usage, and diction are used appropriately for this grade level, with few problems.	Inconsistent use of standard English sentence and paragraph structure, grammar, usage, and diction disrupts readers' comprehension.	Minimal use of standard English sentence and paragraph structure, grammar, usage, and diction confuses the readers.

62 Holt Assessment: Writing, Listening, and Speaking

NAME _____ CLASS _____ DATE _____

for **COLLECTION 4** *page 320*

ANALYTICAL SCALE

Writing: Comparing Media Coverage

Use the chart below (and the rubric on pages 64–65) to evaluate a comparison of media coverage. Circle the numbers that best indicate how well the criteria are met. With these eleven criteria, the lowest possible score is 0, the highest 44.

4 = Clearly meets this criterion
3 = Makes a serious effort to meet this criterion and is fairly successful
2 = Makes some effort to meet this criterion but with little success
1 = Does not achieve this criterion
0 = Unscorable

CRITERIA FOR EVALUATION	RATINGS
Genre, Organization, and Focus	
Opening engages readers' attention.	4 3 2 1
News event and media to be compared and contrasted are introduced.	4 3 2 1
Thesis includes conclusion about media coverage.	4 3 2 1
Organizational pattern (block or point-by-point) is obvious and easy to follow.	4 3 2 1
Similarities and differences are discussed.	4 3 2 1
Each point of comparison is adequately supported.	4 3 2 1
Transitional words and phrases guide the readers.	4 3 2 1
Conclusion mentions factors that might account for similarities and differences.	4 3 2 1
Conclusion reminds readers of thesis and leaves them with an idea to consider.	4 3 2 1
Language Conventions	
Standard English spelling, punctuation, capitalization, and manuscript form are used appropriately for this grade level.	4 3 2 1
Standard English sentence and paragraph structure, grammar, usage, and diction are used appropriately for this grade level.	4 3 2 1
Total Points:	

Workshop Scales and Rubrics **63**

NAME _____ CLASS _____ DATE _____

for **COLLECTION 4** page 320

ANALYTICAL SCORING RUBRIC

Writing: Comparing Media Coverage

WORKSHOP SCALES AND RUBRICS

CRITERIA FOR EVALUATION	SCORE POINT 4	SCORE POINT 3	SCORE POINT 2	SCORE POINT 1
Genre, Organization, and Focus				
Opening engages readers' attention.	Introduction cleverly engages readers' attention with a startling fact, interesting quotation, or intriguing question.	Introduction takes readers into account but does not adequately grab their attention.	Introduction is about the topic but does not engage readers' attention.	Introduction is uninteresting.
News event and media to be compared and contrasted are introduced.	News event and media to be compared and contrasted (the two news media and the news event) are plainly introduced.	News event and media to be compared and contrasted are introduced, but their connection is not clear.	A single news media or news event is mentioned.	No mention is made of news event and media to be compared and contrasted.
Thesis includes conclusion about media coverage.	Thesis or conclusion about the media coverage is stated clearly and coherently in introduction.	Thesis is stated but does not clearly include the conclusion about the media coverage.	A vague or confusing thesis is stated in introduction.	Introduction lacks a thesis.
Organizational pattern (block or point-by-point) is obvious and easy to follow.	Organizational pattern (block or point-by-point) is obvious and easy to follow and is appropriate for the complexity of the comparisons.	Organizational pattern (block or point-by-point) is easy to follow.	Organizational pattern (block or point-by-point) is not maintained throughout the essay.	Organizational pattern is confusing.
Similarities and differences are discussed.	All similarities and differences are explicitly discussed.	Similarities and differences are discussed in general terms.	The distinction between similarities and differences is not made clear.	Little attention to similarities and differences is given; essay is mainly descriptive.
Each point of comparison is adequately supported.	Each point of comparison is adequately supported with specific details, references to a news story, and elaboration from media sources.	Each point of comparison is supported with specific details and references but little elaboration.	Support for points of comparison is sparse or not from media sources.	Support is lacking for points of comparison.

64 Holt Assessment: Writing, Listening, and Speaking

NAME _____ CLASS _____ DATE _____

for COLLECTION 4 *continued*   **ANALYTICAL SCORING RUBRIC**

CRITERIA FOR EVALUATION	SCORE POINT 4	SCORE POINT 3	SCORE POINT 2	SCORE POINT 1
Transitional words and phrases guide the readers.	Carefully chosen transitional words and phrases make the points of comparison clear and guide the readers to connect ideas.	Several appropriate transitional words and phrases guide the readers.	Few transitional words and phrases are used.	Transitional words are missing or inappropriate.
Conclusion mentions factors that might account for similarities and differences.	Conclusion mentions logical factors that might account for similarities and differences.	Conclusion mentions somewhat reasonable factors that might account for similarities and differences.	Conclusion mentions a single factor or far-fetched factors that might account for similarities and differences.	Conclusion ignores factors that might account for similarities and differences.
Conclusion reminds readers of thesis and leaves them with an idea to consider.	Conclusion clearly reminds readers of thesis and leaves them with an idea to consider.	Conclusion reminds readers of thesis or leaves them with an idea to consider.	Conclusion only alludes to thesis.	Essay ends abruptly without concluding statements.
Language Conventions				
Standard English spelling, punctuation, capitalization, and manuscript form are used appropriately for this grade level.	Standard English spelling, punctuation, capitalization, and manuscript form are used appropriately for this grade level throughout the essay.	Standard English spelling, punctuation, capitalization, and manuscript form are used appropriately for this grade level, with few problems.	Inconsistent use of standard English spelling, punctuation, capitalization, and manuscript form disrupts readers' comprehension.	Minimal use of standard English spelling, punctuation, capitalization, and manuscript form confuses the readers.
Standard English sentence and paragraph structure, grammar, usage, and diction are used appropriately for this grade level.	Standard English sentence and paragraph structure, grammar, usage, and diction are used appropriately for this grade level throughout the essay.	Standard English sentence and paragraph structure, grammar, usage, and diction are used appropriately for this grade level, with few problems.	Inconsistent use of standard English sentence and paragraph structure, grammar, usage, and diction disrupts readers' comprehension.	Minimal use of standard English sentence and paragraph structure, grammar, usage, and diction confuses the readers.

WORKSHOP SCALES AND RUBRICS

Workshop Scales and Rubrics **65**

NAME _____ CLASS _____ DATE _____

for COLLECTION 5 *page 382*

ANALYTICAL SCALE

Writing: Persuasive Essay

Use the chart below (and the rubric on pages 67–68) to evaluate a persuasive essay. Circle the numbers that best indicate how well the criteria are met. With twelve criteria, the lowest possible score is 0, the highest 48.

4 = Clearly meets this criterion
3 = Makes a serious effort to meet this criterion and is fairly successful
2 = Makes some effort to meet this criterion but with little success
1 = Does not achieve this criterion
0 = Unscorable

CRITERIA FOR EVALUATION	RATING
Genre, Organization, and Focus	
Introduction grabs readers' interest.	4 3 2 1
Introduction gives background information.	4 3 2 1
Opinion statement identifies the issue and states opinion.	4 3 2 1
At least three reasons support the opinion statement.	4 3 2 1
At least two pieces of evidence support each reason.	4 3 2 1
Organization of reasons and evidence is logical and effective.	4 3 2 1
Possible counterclaims of readers are addressed.	4 3 2 1
Conclusion restates opinion.	4 3 2 1
Conclusion includes a summary of reasons or a call to action.	4 3 2 1
Original expressions replace clichés.	4 3 2 1
Language Conventions	
Standard English spelling, punctuation, capitalization, and manuscript form are used appropriately for this grade level.	4 3 2 1
Standard English sentence and paragraph structure, grammar, usage, and diction are used appropriately for this grade level.	4 3 2 1
Total Points:	

WORKSHOP SCALES AND RUBRICS

NAME _____ CLASS _____ DATE _____

for **COLLECTION 5** *page 382*

ANALYTICAL SCORING RUBRIC

Writing: Persuasive Essay

CRITERIA FOR EVALUATION	SCORE POINT 4	SCORE POINT 3	SCORE POINT 2	SCORE POINT 1
Genre, Organization, and Focus				
Introduction grabs readers' interest.	Introduction grabs readers' interest with an attention getter.	Introduction takes readers into account but does not grab their attention.	Introduction is relevant but only partially addresses readers' interests.	Introduction is dull or uninteresting.
Introduction gives background information.	Introduction includes relevant and solid background information that helps readers understand the issue and make a decision.	Introduction includes some background information that helps readers partially understand the issue.	Introduction includes scant background information that is little help to readers.	Background information is absent or irrelevant.
Opinion statement identifies the issue and states opinion.	Opinion statement identifies a well-defined issue and a clear opinion.	Opinion statement identifies the issue and opinion but lacks clarity.	Opinion statement vaguely identifies the issue or opinion.	An opinion statement cannot be identified.
At least three reasons support the opinion statement.	At least three strong reasons that appeal to readers' logic, emotions, or ethical beliefs support the opinion statement.	At least three reasons that appeal to readers' logic, emotions, or ethical beliefs support the opinion statement.	Fewer than three reasons support the opinion statement, or reasons rely on only one type of appeal.	A single reason supports the opinion statement, or reasons are unrelated to opinion statement.
At least two pieces of evidence support each reason.	At least two pieces of relevant, specific, and precise evidence support each reason and present a tightly reasoned argument.	At least two pieces of relevant evidence support each reason.	Sparse evidence is vague and partially relevant, or each reason is not supported.	Evidence is irrelevant or missing.
Organization of reasons and evidence is logical and effective.	Organization is effective as each idea moves smoothly and logically to the next, with the strongest reasons at the beginning or end.	Each idea is logically connected to the next.	Organization is unclear, and several ideas do not move logically from one to another.	Organization is illogical and confusing.

Workshop Scales and Rubrics **67**

for **COLLECTION 5** continued

ANALYTICAL SCORING RUBRIC

CRITERIA FOR EVALUATION	SCORE POINT 4	SCORE POINT 3	SCORE POINT 2	SCORE POINT 1
Possible counter-claims of readers are addressed.	Reasons and evidence sufficiently address possible counterclaims, concerns, or biases of readers.	Reasons and evidence partially address possible counterclaims of readers.	Possible counter-claims of readers are acknowledged but not addressed.	No possible counterclaims of readers are addressed.
Conclusion restates opinion.	Conclusion clearly and accurately restates opinion.	Conclusion loosely restates opinion.	Conclusion only hints at opinion.	Conclusion omits restatement of opinion.
Conclusion includes a summary of reasons or a call to action.	Conclusion includes a clear, succinct summary, or the call to action tells readers exactly what to do.	Conclusion includes a general summary or suggests a call to action.	Conclusion hints at reasons or vaguely suggests a call to action.	Conclusion omits summary of reasons or call to action.
Original expressions replace clichés.	Fresh, original expressions replace clichés.	Several original expressions replace clichés.	Clichés are sprinkled throughout essay.	Many clichés are evident throughout essay.
Language Conventions				
Standard English spelling, punctuation, capitalization, and manuscript form are used appropriately for this grade level.	Standard English spelling, punctuation, capitalization, and manuscript form are used appropriately for this grade level throughout the essay.	Standard English spelling, punctuation, capitalization, and manuscript form are used appropriately for this grade level, with few problems.	Inconsistent use of standard English spelling, punctuation, capitalization, and manuscript form disrupts readers' comprehension.	Minimal use of standard English spelling, punctuation, capitalization, and manuscript form confuses the readers.
Standard English sentence and paragraph structure, grammar, usage, and diction are used appropriately for this grade level.	Standard English sentence and paragraph structure, grammar, usage, and diction are used appropriately for this grade level throughout the essay.	Standard English sentence and paragraph structure, grammar, usage, and diction are used appropriately for this grade level, with few problems.	Inconsistent use of standard English sentence and paragraph structure, grammar, usage, and diction disrupts readers' comprehension.	Minimal use of standard English sentence and paragraph structure, grammar, usage, and diction confuses the readers.

NAME _____ CLASS _____ DATE _____

for **COLLECTION 5** *page 390*

ANALYTICAL SCALE

Listening and Speaking: Conducting a Debate

Use the chart below to evaluate a debate. Circle the numbers that best indicate how well the criteria are met. With these eight criteria for participating in a debate, the lowest possible score is 0, the highest 32.

4 = Clearly meets this criterion
3 = Makes a serious effort to meet this criterion and is fairly successful
2 = Makes some effort to meet this criterion but with little success
1 = Does not achieve this criterion
0 = Unscorable

CRITERIA FOR EVALUATION	RATINGS
Content, Organization, and Delivery	
Key issues are identified (existence of problem, causes, proposition to solve problem, and cost of proposition).	4 3 2 1
Speeches employ classical speech form (brief but engaging introduction, smooth transitions, concise body, and strong conclusion).	4 3 2 1
Specific reasons support arguments.	4 3 2 1
Credible, valid, and relevant evidence (specific instances, testimony, facts, and statistics) supports each reason.	4 3 2 1
Constructive speeches build the argument in favor of proposition or defend the way things are.	4 3 2 1
Rebuttal speeches refute quantity and quality of evidence and logic of opponent's reasoning, or they rebuild own argument.	4 3 2 1
Delivery (voice, facial expressions, gestures, volume, rate, eye contact, and etiquette) makes message expressive.	4 3 2 1
Language Conventions	
Standard English grammar, usage, and diction are used appropriately for this grade level.	4 3 2 1
Total Points:	

for **COLLECTION 5** page 390

ANALYTICAL SCALE

Listening and Speaking: Judging a Debate

Use the chart below to evaluate how students judge a debate. Circle the numbers that best indicate how well the criteria are met. For judging a debate, with six criteria the lowest possible score is 0, the highest 24.

4 = Clearly meets this criterion
3 = Makes a serious effort to meet this criterion and is fairly successful
2 = Makes some effort to meet this criterion but with little success
1 = Does not achieve this criterion
0 = Unscorable

CRITERIA FOR EVALUATION	RATINGS
The Listener	
Evaluates whether a speaker or team demonstrates that a significant problem does or does not exist and identifies how thoroughly a team has analyzed the problem.	4 3 2 1
Evaluates how effectively a speaker or team proves that a proposition is or is not a problem's best solution.	4 3 2 1
Identifies effectiveness of reasons and credibility, validity, and relevance of evidence.	4 3 2 1
Evaluates effectiveness of refutations and rebuttal arguments.	4 3 2 1
Evaluates delivery (eye contact, appropriate rate and volume, confidence, thorough preparation, and proper debate etiquette).	4 3 2 1
Evaluates standard English grammar, usage, and diction.	4 3 2 1
Total Points:	

70 Holt Assessment: Writing, Listening, and Speaking

NAME	CLASS	DATE

for **COLLECTION 6** *page 456*

ANALYTICAL SCALE

Writing: Describing a Place

Use the chart below (and the rubric on pages 72–73) to evaluate a descriptive essay. Circle the numbers that best indicate how well the criteria are met. With these nine criteria, the lowest possible score is 0, the highest 36.

4 = Clearly meets this criterion
3 = Makes a serious effort to meet this criterion and is fairly successful
2 = Makes some effort to meet this criterion but with little success
1 = Does not achieve this criterion
0 = Unscorable

CRITERIA FOR EVALUATION	RATING
Genre, Organization, and Focus	
Introduction grabs readers' attention.	4 3 2 1
Introduction states the controlling impression and makes the subject and point of view clear.	4 3 2 1
The description includes a variety of sensory, factual, and figurative details.	4 3 2 1
Details about the writer's thoughts and feelings are included.	4 3 2 1
Details are organized in spatial order or order of importance.	4 3 2 1
Adjectives are descriptive but not repetitive.	4 3 2 1
Conclusion sums up thoughts about the place and restates controlling impression.	4 3 2 1
Language Conventions	
Standard English spelling, punctuation, capitalization, and manuscript form are used appropriately for this grade level.	4 3 2 1
Standard English sentence and paragraph structure, grammar, usage, and diction are used appropriately for this grade level.	4 3 2 1
Total Points:	

WORKSHOP SCALES AND RUBRICS

Workshop Scales and Rubrics

NAME _____ CLASS _____ DATE _____

for **COLLECTION 6** page 456   **ANALYTICAL SCORING RUBRIC**

Writing: Describing a Place

CRITERIA FOR EVALUATION	SCORE POINT 4	SCORE POINT 3	SCORE POINT 2	SCORE POINT 1
Genre, Organization, and Focus				
Introduction grabs the readers' attention.	Introduction grabs readers' attention with a question or interesting statement.	Introduction takes readers into account but does not adequately grab their attention.	Introduction is about the topic, but does not engage readers' attention.	Introduction is dull.
Introduction states the controlling impression and makes the writer's point of view clear.	Introduction states the controlling impression explicitly and makes the writer's point of view clear.	Introduction states the controlling impression and the writer's point of view, but they lack clarity.	The controlling impression and writer's point of view in the introduction are so subtle or ambiguous that they are difficult to determine.	Introduction lacks a controlling impression and a definite point of view.
The description includes a variety of sensory, factual, and figurative details.	The description includes a variety of vivid sensory, factual, and figurative details.	The description includes sensory, factual, and figurative details, but some are trite.	Few sensory, factual, and figurative details are included.	Sensory, factual, or figurative details are sparse or unrelated to the place described.
Details about the writer's thoughts and feelings are included.	Appropriately placed details about the writer's thoughts and feelings clearly express the writer's attitude.	Several clear details about the writer's thoughts and feelings are included.	Few details about the writer's thoughts and feelings are included, making the essay feel impersonal.	Details about the writer's thoughts and feelings are missing, or the essay is almost entirely thoughts and feelings about the place.
Details are organized in spatial order or order of importance.	Organization of details in spatial order or order of importance makes sense to readers.	Details are organized in spatial order or order of importance, with few lapses.	Organization of details shifts abruptly from spatial order or order of importance in the essay.	Organization is unclear.
Adjectives are descriptive but not repetitive.	Adjectives are descriptive and precise.	Adjectives are mostly descriptive, but a few pointlessly repeat the same meaning.	Adjectives are frequently in repetitive pairs, weakening the description.	Adjectives are sparse, overabundant, or repetitive.

WORKSHOP SCALES AND RUBRICS

72   Holt Assessment: Writing, Listening, and Speaking

NAME _____ CLASS _____ DATE _____

for **COLLECTION 6** *continued* **ANALYTICAL SCORING RUBRIC**

CRITERIA FOR EVALUATION	SCORE POINT 4	SCORE POINT 3	SCORE POINT 2	SCORE POINT 1
Conclusion sums up thoughts about the place and restates controlling impression.	Conclusion succinctly sums up thoughts about the place and clearly restates controlling impression.	Conclusion gives thoughts about the place and restates controlling impression, but conclusion wanders or is too brief.	Conclusion either sums up thoughts about the place or restates controlling impression, but not both.	Essay ends abruptly, or conclusion lacks a summary and controlling impression.
Language Conventions				
Standard English spelling, punctuation, capitalization, and manuscript form are used appropriately for this grade level.	Standard English spelling, punctuation, capitalization, and manuscript form are used appropriately for this grade level throughout the essay.	Standard English spelling, punctuation, capitalization, and manuscript form are used appropriately for this grade level, with few problems.	Inconsistent use of standard English spelling, punctuation, capitalization, and manuscript form disrupts readers' comprehension.	Minimal use of standard English spelling, punctuation, capitalization, and manuscript form confuses the readers.
Standard English sentence and paragraph structure, grammar, usage, and diction are used appropriately for this grade level.	Standard English sentence and paragraph structure, grammar, usage, and diction are used appropriately for this grade level throughout the essay.	Standard English sentence and paragraph structure, grammar, usage, and diction are used appropriately for this grade level, with few problems.	Inconsistent use of standard English sentence and paragraph structure, grammar, usage, and diction disrupts readers' comprehension.	Minimal use of standard English sentence and paragraph structure, grammar, usage, and diction confuses the readers.

Workshop Scales and Rubrics

NAME _____ CLASS _____ DATE _____

for **COLLECTION 6** page 464

ANALYTICAL SCALE

Speaking: Presenting a Description

Use the chart below to evaluate a descriptive presentation. Circle the numbers that best indicate how well the criteria are met. With these nine criteria, the lowest possible score is 0, the highest 36.

4 = Clearly meets this criterion
3 = Makes a serious effort to meet this criterion and is fairly successful
2 = Makes some effort to meet this criterion but with little success
1 = Does not achieve this criterion
0 = Unscorable

CRITERIA FOR EVALUATION	RATING
Content, Organization, and Delivery	
Introduction states the controlling impression.	4 3 2 1
Concrete imagery helps listeners create mental images of the place described.	4 3 2 1
Sensory, factual, figurative details and shifting vantage points and perspectives help audience visualize the place described from more than one viewpoint.	4 3 2 1
Thoughts and feelings show personal involvement with the subject.	4 3 2 1
Details are organized in spatial order or order of importance.	4 3 2 1
Visuals are incorporated into description and appeal to interests of audience.	4 3 2 1
Verbal and nonverbal techniques communicate message to audience.	4 3 2 1
If used, notes (on cards) facilitate delivery.	4 3 2 1
Language Conventions	
Standard English is used appropriately for this grade level.	4 3 2 1
Total Points:	

WORKSHOP SCALES AND RUBRICS

74   Holt Assessment: Writing, Listening, and Speaking

NAME _____ CLASS _____ DATE _____

for **COLLECTION 7** page 556

ANALYTICAL SCALE

Writing: Analyzing a Poem

Use the chart below (and the rubric on pages 76–77) to evaluate an analysis of a poem. Circle the numbers that best indicate how well the criteria are met. With these ten criteria, the lowest possible score is 0, the highest 40.

4 = Clearly meets this criterion
3 = Makes a serious effort to meet this criterion and is fairly successful
2 = Makes some effort to meet this criterion but with little success
1 = Does not achieve this criterion
0 = Unscorable

CRITERIA FOR EVALUATION	RATING
Genre, Organization, and Focus	
Introduction grabs readers' attention.	4 3 2 1
Introduction includes poem's title and author and a clear thesis.	4 3 2 1
Each body paragraph discusses and elaborates a key literary element that supports the thesis.	4 3 2 1
Each key literary element is supported with references to the poem.	4 3 2 1
Key literary elements are organized by order of importance or in the order they appear in the poem.	4 3 2 1
A lack of wordy, unnecessary clauses contributes to a knowledgeable, friendly tone.	4 3 2 1
Conclusion reminds readers of thesis and summarizes main points.	4 3 2 1
Conclusion shows how the poem relates to broader themes in life.	4 3 2 1
Language Conventions	
Standard English spelling, punctuation, capitalization, and manuscript form are used appropriately for this grade level.	4 3 2 1
Standard English sentence and paragraph structure, grammar, usage, and diction are used appropriately for this grade level.	4 3 2 1
Total Points:	

Workshop Scales and Rubrics

NAME _____ CLASS _____ DATE _____

for **COLLECTION 7** page 556

ANALYTICAL SCORING RUBRIC

Writing: Analyzing a Poem

WORKSHOP SCALES AND RUBRICS

Genre, Organization, and Focus

CRITERIA FOR EVALUATION	SCORE POINT 4	SCORE POINT 3	SCORE POINT 2	SCORE POINT 1
Introduction grabs readers' attention.	Introduction grabs readers' attention by relating poem's meaning to experiences people have in common.	Introduction takes readers into account but does not adequately grab their attention.	Introduction is about the topic but does not engage readers' attention.	Introduction is uninteresting.
Introduction includes poem's title and author and a clear thesis.	Introduction includes poem's title and author and a clear thesis that identifies key literary elements and the poem's theme.	Introduction includes poem's title and author and a thesis, but thesis gives only key literary elements or the theme, but not both.	Introduction includes poem's title or author, but thesis is difficult to identify.	Title and author or thesis is missing.
Each body paragraph discusses and elaborates a key literary element that supports the thesis.	Each body paragraph discusses and elaborates on a key literary element that supports the thesis by addressing ambiguities, nuances, or complexities.	Each body paragraph discusses and elaborates on a key literary element that supports the thesis to some degree, but explanation of ambiguities, nuances, or complexities is limited.	Few body paragraphs are elaborated, or explanations provide little support for thesis.	Body paragraphs discuss more than one literary element, thesis is unsupported, and/or explanations and elaboration are sparse.
Each key literary element is supported with references to the poem.	Each key literary element is supported with references (quotations and restated details) to the poem.	Most key literary elements are supported with references to the poem, but a significant imbalance between quotations and restated details exists.	Key literary elements have little support from references to the poem.	References to the poem are missing.
Key literary elements are organized by order of importance or in the order they appear in the poem.	Key literary elements are clearly organized by order of importance or in the order they appear in the poem.	Key literary elements are largely organized by order of importance or in the order they appear in the poem.	Order of key literary elements is difficult to determine because organization shifts.	Order of key literary elements appears random.

76 Holt Assessment: Writing, Listening, and Speaking

NAME _____ CLASS _____ DATE _____

for **COLLECTION 7** *continued* **ANALYTICAL SCORING RUBRIC**

CRITERIA FOR EVALUATION	SCORE POINT 4	SCORE POINT 3	SCORE POINT 2	SCORE POINT 1
A lack of wordy, unnecessary clauses contributes to a knowledgeable, friendly tone.	Participles or participial phrases replace unnecessary clauses in wordy sentences and contribute to a knowledgeable, friendly tone.	A few wordy, unnecessary clauses detract from a knowledgeable, friendly tone.	Overuse of wordy, unnecessary clauses detracts from the message of the analysis.	Wordy, unnecessary clauses make the analysis difficult to read.
Conclusion reminds readers of thesis and summarizes main points.	Conclusion effectively reminds readers of thesis and succinctly summarizes main points.	Conclusion reminds readers of thesis and summarizes main points, but lacks some clarity.	Conclusion either restates thesis or names a main point, but not both.	Conclusion rambles and lacks a reminder of thesis or summary of main points, or the analysis ends abruptly.
Conclusion shows how the poem relates to broader themes in life.	Conclusion shows how the poem directly relates to broader themes in life.	Conclusion somewhat shows how the poem relates to broader themes in life.	Conclusion mentions a theme in life, but it has little relationship to poem.	Conclusion ignores broader themes in life.

Language Conventions

Standard English spelling, punctuation, capitalization, and manuscript form are used appropriately for this grade level.	Standard English spelling, punctuation, capitalization, and manuscript form are used appropriately for this grade level throughout the essay.	Standard English spelling, punctuation, capitalization, and manuscript form are used appropriately for this grade level, with few problems.	Inconsistent use of standard English spelling, punctuation, capitalization, and manuscript form disrupts readers' comprehension.	Minimal use of standard English spelling, punctuation, capitalization, and manuscript form confuses the readers.
Standard English sentence and paragraph structure, grammar, usage, and diction are used appropriately for this grade level.	Standard English sentence and paragraph structure, grammar, usage, and diction are used appropriately for this grade level throughout the essay.	Standard English sentence and paragraph structure, grammar, usage, and diction are used appropriately for this grade level, with few problems.	Inconsistent use of standard English sentence and paragraph structure, grammar, usage, and diction disrupts readers' comprehension.	Minimal use of standard English sentence and paragraph structure, grammar, usage, and diction confuses the readers.

WORKSHOP SCALES AND RUBRICS

Workshop Scales and Rubrics

NAME _____ CLASS _____ DATE _____

for COLLECTION 7 page 564

ANALYTICAL SCALE

Speaking: Presenting a Poem

Use the chart below to evaluate an oral presentation of a poem. Circle the numbers that best indicate how well the criteria are met. With these six criteria, the lowest possible score is 0, the highest 24.

4 = Clearly meets this criterion
3 = Makes a serious effort to meet this criterion and is fairly successful
2 = Makes some effort to meet this criterion but with little success
1 = Does not achieve this criterion
0 = Unscorable

CRITERIA FOR EVALUATION	RATINGS
Content, Organization, and Delivery	
Diction is clear and careful and helps listeners understand the poem.	4 3 2 1
Emphasis of key words and phrases increases effectiveness of delivery.	4 3 2 1
Pauses help listeners understand the meaning of the poem.	4 3 2 1
Eye contact communicates confidence and sincerity.	4 3 2 1
Facial expressions help convey the meaning of the poem.	4 3 2 1
Relaxed, natural gestures increase effectiveness of delivery.	4 3 2 1
Total Points:	

WORKSHOP SCALES AND RUBRICS

78   Holt Assessment: Writing, Listening, and Speaking

NAME _____ CLASS _____ DATE _____

for **COLLECTION 8** *page 630*

ANALYTICAL SCALE

Writing: Analyzing a Short Story

Use the chart below (and the rubric on pages 80–81) to evaluate an analysis of a short story. Circle the numbers that best indicate how well the criteria are met. With these eleven criteria, the lowest possible score is 0, the highest 44.

4 = Clearly meets this criterion
3 = Makes a serious effort to meet this criterion and is fairly successful
2 = Makes some effort to meet this criterion but with little success
1 = Does not achieve this criterion
0 = Unscorable

CRITERIA FOR EVALUATION	RATINGS
Genre, Organization, and Focus	
Introduction identifies title and author of story.	4 3 2 1
Introduction grabs readers' attention.	4 3 2 1
Thesis presents the focus element and key points.	4 3 2 1
Each body paragraph discusses one key point that supports the thesis.	4 3 2 1
Evidence from the text supports each key point.	4 3 2 1
Elaboration explains how the evidence supports each key point.	4 3 2 1
Conclusion restates the thesis.	4 3 2 1
Conclusion summarizes key points.	4 3 2 1
A final comment connects the analysis to real life.	4 3 2 1
Language Conventions	
Standard English spelling, punctuation, capitalization, and manuscript form are used appropriately for this grade level.	4 3 2 1
Standard English sentence and paragraph structure, grammar, usage (with a focus on appropriate modifiers), and diction are used appropriately for this grade level.	4 3 2 1
Total Points:	

WORKSHOP SCALES AND RUBRICS

Workshop Scales and Rubrics

NAME _____ CLASS _____ DATE _____

for **COLLECTION 8** page 630

ANALYTICAL SCORING RUBRIC

Writing: Analyzing a Short Story

CRITERIA FOR EVALUATION	SCORE POINT 4	SCORE POINT 3	SCORE POINT 2	SCORE POINT 1
Genre, Organization, and Focus				
Introduction identifies title and author of story.	Introduction accurately identifies complete title and author of story.	Introduction identifies title and author of story, but one is not complete.	Introduction identifies either title or author of story.	Title and author are omitted.
Introduction grabs readers' attention.	Introduction grabs readers' attention by relating an anecdote or asking a question.	Introduction takes readers into account but does not adequately grab their attention.	Introduction is about the topic but does not grab readers' attention.	Introduction is uninteresting.
Thesis presents the focus element and key points.	Thesis presents the focus element and key points and plainly indicates how they work together.	Thesis presents the focus element and key points, but they are not clearly linked.	Thesis presents the focus element but does not identify key points.	Thesis is not stated.
Each body paragraph discusses one key point.	Each body paragraph distinctly discusses one key point.	Most body paragraphs discuss one key point to some extent.	Most body paragraphs discuss more than one key point.	Body paragraphs fragment key points into several miniature paragraphs, or entire analysis is a single paragraph.
Evidence from the text supports each key point.	Evidence from the text directly supports each key point with direct quotations, paraphrases, or summaries.	Evidence from the text supports several key points, but it is not always in the appropriate form.	Very little evidence from the text supports key points.	Evidence from the text is not included.
Elaboration explains how the evidence supports each key point.	Elaboration clearly explains how the evidence supports each key point and what it means.	Elaboration tells how the evidence supports each key point.	Elaboration does not clarify connections between evidence and key points.	Elaboration does not relate to key points or does not exist.
Conclusion restates the thesis.	Conclusion restates the thesis in a fresh way.	Restatement of thesis mimics original thesis.	Restatement of thesis is confusing or is inconsistent with original thesis.	Conclusion lacks a restatement of thesis.

WORKSHOP SCALES AND RUBRICS

80 Holt Assessment: Writing, Listening, and Speaking

NAME _____ CLASS _____ DATE _____

for COLLECTION 8 *continued* **ANALYTICAL SCORING RUBRIC**

CRITERIA FOR EVALUATION	SCORE POINT 4	SCORE POINT 3	SCORE POINT 2	SCORE POINT 1
Conclusion summarizes key points.	Conclusion succinctly summarizes all key points.	Conclusion summarizes most key points.	Summary of key points rambles or is too brief to be meaningful.	A summary of key points is missing.
A final comment connects the analysis to real life.	A thoughtful, final comment connects the analysis closely to real life.	A final comment somewhat connects the analysis to real life.	A final comment is made about real life but is not connected to the analysis.	A connection to real life is not made.
Language Conventions				
Standard English spelling, punctuation, capitalization, and manuscript form are used appropriately for this grade level.	Standard English spelling, punctuation, capitalization, and manuscript form are used appropriately for this grade level throughout the essay.	Standard English spelling, punctuation, capitalization, and manuscript form are used appropriately for this grade level, with few problems.	Inconsistent use of standard English spelling, punctuation, capitalization, and manuscript form disrupts readers' comprehension.	Minimal use of standard English spelling, punctuation, capitalization, and manuscript form confuses the readers.
Standard English sentence and paragraph structure, grammar, usage (with a focus on appropriate modifiers), and diction are used appropriately for this grade level.	Standard English sentence and paragraph structure, grammar, usage (with a focus on appropriate modifiers), and diction are used appropriately for this grade level throughout the essay.	Standard English sentence and paragraph structure, grammar, usage (with a focus on appropriate modifiers), and diction are used appropriately for this grade level, with few problems.	Inconsistent use of standard English sentence and paragraph structure, grammar, usage, and diction disrupts readers' comprehension.	Minimal use of standard English sentence and paragraph structure, grammar, usage, and diction confuses the readers.

WORKSHOP SCALES AND RUBRICS

Workshop Scales and Rubrics **81**

NAME _____ CLASS _____ DATE _____

for **COLLECTION 9** page 706

ANALYTICAL SCALE

Writing: Research Paper

Use the chart below (and the rubric on pages 83–84) to evaluate a research paper. Circle the numbers that best indicate how well the criteria are met. With these twelve criteria, the lowest possible score is 0, the highest 48.

4 = Clearly meets this criterion
3 = Makes a serious effort to meet this criterion and is fairly successful
2 = Makes some effort to meet this criterion but with little success
1 = Does not achieve this criterion
0 = Unscorable

CRITERIA FOR EVALUATION	RATING
Genre, Organization, and Focus	
Introduction captures readers' attention.	4 3 2 1
Background information on the topic is supplied.	4 3 2 1
Thesis statement answers the research question.	4 3 2 1
Separate body paragraphs develop each main point.	4 3 2 1
Each main point is supported with evidence.	4 3 2 1
Main points and evidence are in a logical order.	4 3 2 1
Direct quotations, paraphrases, and summaries are smoothly integrated into the paper.	4 3 2 1
All sources are given proper credit.	4 3 2 1
Conclusion restates the thesis.	4 3 2 1
Paper ends with a closing thought.	4 3 2 1
Language Conventions	
Standard English spelling, punctuation, capitalization, and manuscript form are used appropriately for this grade level.	4 3 2 1
Standard English sentence and paragraph structure (with an emphasis on varied sentence beginnings), grammar, usage, and diction are used appropriately for this grade level.	4 3 2 1
Total Points:	

WORKSHOP SCALES AND RUBRICS

Holt Assessment: Writing, Listening, and Speaking

NAME _____ CLASS _____ DATE _____

for **COLLECTION 9** *page 706* **ANALYTICAL SCORING RUBRIC**

Writing: Research Paper

CRITERIA FOR EVALUATION	SCORE POINT 4	SCORE POINT 3	SCORE POINT 2	SCORE POINT 1
Genre, Organization, and Focus				
Introduction captures readers' attention.	Introduction captures readers' attention with a question, anecdote, or interesting fact.	Introduction takes readers into account but does not adequately capture their attention.	Introduction is relevant to topic but does not take the interests of audience into account.	Introduction is dull and uninviting.
Background information on the topic is supplied.	Background information on the topic is supplied and tailored to the audience.	Background information on the topic is supplied, but only some is tailored to audience.	Very little background information on the topic is supplied, or it ignores needs of audience.	No background information is supplied.
Thesis statement answers the research question.	Thesis statement clearly answers the specific research question.	Thesis turns the research question into a statement but does not add information.	Thesis is the research question.	Thesis is missing.
Separate body paragraphs develop each main point.	Separate body paragraphs distinctly develop each main point.	Separate body paragraphs develop main points, although more than one main point appears occasionally in a single paragraph.	Body paragraphs often contain more than one main point.	Body paragraphs fragment main points into several miniature paragraphs, or entire body is a single paragraph or two.
Each main point is supported with evidence.	Each main point is well supported with evidence (facts and details).	Each main point is supported with evidence, but evidence for some points is not sufficient.	Some main points are supported with evidence, but evidence is sparse.	Evidence for main points is lacking.
Main points and evidence are in a logical order.	Main points and evidence are clearly and logically organized for the topic—chronological, logical, or order of importance.	Main points and evidence are generally in a logical order.	A few main points and evidence are in a logical order, but many points or evidence seem out of place.	Order of research paper is random and confusing to the readers.

WORKSHOP SCALES AND RUBRICS

Workshop Scales and Rubrics **83**

NAME _____ CLASS _____ DATE _____

for COLLECTION 9 continued   **ANALYTICAL SCORING RUBRIC**

CRITERIA FOR EVALUATION	SCORE POINT 4	SCORE POINT 3	SCORE POINT 2	SCORE POINT 1
Direct quotations, paraphrases, and summaries are smoothly integrated into the paper.	Direct quotations, paraphrases, and summaries are smoothly and effectively integrated into the paper.	Most direct quotations, paraphrases, and summaries are smoothly integrated into the paper.	Direct quotations, paraphrases, and summaries are abrupt or jarring.	Direct quotations, paraphrases, and summaries are jumbled together.
All sources are given proper credit.	All sources are given proper credit both within the text and in the Works Cited list.	Most sources are given proper credit, but sometimes the source is only in the text or only in the Works Cited list.	Few sources are given credit, either in the text or in the Works Cited list.	References to sources are not made.
Conclusion restates the thesis.	Conclusion restates the thesis in different words.	Restatement of thesis mimics original thesis.	Restatement of thesis is confusing or is inconsistent with original thesis.	Conclusion lacks a restatement of thesis.
Paper ends with a closing thought.	Paper ends with a pertinent, engaging closing thought, idea, or point to ponder.	Paper ends with a suitable closing thought.	Closing thought is not tightly linked to topic.	Paper ends abruptly.

▶ **Language Conventions**

	SCORE POINT 4	SCORE POINT 3	SCORE POINT 2	SCORE POINT 1
Standard English spelling, punctuation, capitalization, and manuscript form are used appropriately for this grade level.	Standard English spelling, punctuation, capitalization, and manuscript form are used appropriately for this grade level throughout the essay.	Standard English spelling, punctuation, capitalization, and manuscript form are used appropriately for this grade level, with few problems.	Inconsistent use of standard English spelling, punctuation, capitalization, and manuscript form disrupts readers' comprehension.	Minimal use of standard English spelling, punctuation, capitalization, and manuscript form confuses the readers.
Standard English sentence and paragraph structure (with an emphasis on varied sentence beginnings), grammar, usage, and diction are used appropriately for this grade level.	Standard English sentence and paragraph structure (with an emphasis on varied sentence beginnings), grammar, usage, and diction are used appropriately for this grade level throughout the essay.	Standard English sentence and paragraph structure (with an emphasis on varied sentence beginnings), grammar, usage, and diction are used appropriately for this grade level, with few problems.	Inconsistent use of standard English sentence and paragraph structure, grammar, usage, and diction disrupts readers' comprehension.	Minimal use of standard English sentence and paragraph structure, grammar, usage, and diction confuses the readers.

Holt Assessment: Writing, Listening, and Speaking

NAME _____ CLASS _____ DATE _____

for **COLLECTION 9** page 726

ANALYTICAL SCALE

Speaking: Presenting Research

Use the chart below to evaluate a research presentation. Circle the numbers that best indicate how well the criteria are met. With these nine criteria, the lowest possible score is 0, the highest 36.

4 = Clearly meets this criterion
3 = Makes a serious effort to meet this criterion and is fairly successful
2 = Makes some effort to meet this criterion but with little success
1 = Does not achieve this criterion
0 = Unscorable

CRITERIA FOR EVALUATION	RATING
Content, Organization, and Delivery	
Introduction grabs listeners' attention with a startling statement, an interesting and relevant anecdote, or a connection to interests of listeners.	4 3 2 1
Ideas are organized in either chronological order or order of importance.	4 3 2 1
Each section begins with a preview and ends with a summary.	4 3 2 1
Use of both primary and secondary sources shows that all important ideas and perspectives are considered.	4 3 2 1
Telling sources of information adds to credibility.	4 3 2 1
Conclusion summarizes main points and ends with an interesting thought or question.	4 3 2 1
Verbal techniques and nonverbal techniques enhance understanding.	4 3 2 1
Visuals or props, if used, enhance the appeal and clarity of presentation.	4 3 2 1
Language Conventions	
Standard English grammar and usage are used appropriately for this grade level.	4 3 2 1
Total Points:	

Workshop Scales and Rubrics

NAME _____ CLASS _____ DATE _____

for **COLLECTION 10** page 834

ANALYTICAL SCALE

Writing: Persuading with Cause and Effect

Use the chart below (and the rubric on pages 87–88) to evaluate a persuasive essay. Circle the numbers that best indicate how well the criteria are met. With these twelve criteria, the lowest possible score is 0, the highest 48.

4 = Clearly meets this criterion
3 = Makes a serious effort to meet this criterion and is fairly successful
2 = Makes some effort to meet this criterion but with little success
1 = Does not achieve this criterion
0 = Unscorable

CRITERIA FOR EVALUATION	RATINGS
Genre, Organization, and Focus	
Essay begins with a bold statement or anecdote.	4 3 2 1
If necessary, background information is provided.	4 3 2 1
Introduction includes clear opinion statement.	4 3 2 1
Cause and effects of the situation are explained.	4 3 2 1
Persuasive appeals are included.	4 3 2 1
A variety of evidence supports explanations.	4 3 2 1
Cause-effect clue words help explain the situation and its negative effects.	4 3 2 1
Conclusion addresses the readers' counterclaims.	4 3 2 1
Conclusion restates opinion statement.	4 3 2 1
Conclusion includes a specific call to action and ends with a strong statement.	4 3 2 1
Language Conventions	
Standard English spelling, punctuation, capitalization, and manuscript form are used appropriately for this grade level.	4 3 2 1
Standard English sentence and paragraph structure, grammar, usage, and diction are used appropriately for this grade level.	4 3 2 1
Total Points:	

WORKSHOP SCALES AND RUBRICS

NAME _____ CLASS _____ DATE _____

for **COLLECTION 10** page 834

ANALYTICAL SCORING RUBRIC

Writing: Persuading with Cause and Effect

CRITERIA FOR EVALUATION	SCORE POINT 4	SCORE POINT 3	SCORE POINT 2	SCORE POINT 1
Genre, Organization, and Focus				
Essay begins with a bold statement or anecdote.	Essay begins with a bold statement or engaging anecdote that grabs readers' attention.	Essay begins with statement or anecdote that interests readers.	Beginning statement or anecdote is bland or unrelated to situation.	Essay begins with dull statement.
If necessary, background information is provided.	If necessary, background information that is directed at specific audience is provided.	If necessary, background information is provided, but it is inappropriate for intended audience.	Background information is unnecessary or insignificant.	No useful background information is provided.
Introduction includes clear opinion statement.	Introduction includes clear opinion statement that indicates writer's perspective and hints at the effects to be discussed.	Introduction includes opinion statement but does not hint at discussion of effects.	Opinion statement is unclear and/or difficult to identify.	Opinion statement is missing.
Cause and effects of the situation are explained.	Cause and significant effects of the situation are convincingly explained.	Cause and effects of the situation are explained without motivating readers.	The cause or a single effect of the situation is explained.	Cause and effects of the situation are ignored.
Persuasive appeals are included.	Appropriate persuasive appeals (logical, emotional, and ethical) are included.	Persuasive appeals are included but are not always appropriate to the explanation.	Persuasive appeals are weak or inappropriate.	Persuasive appeals are not made.
A variety of evidence supports explanations.	A variety of evidence (expert opinions, quotations, facts, anecdotes, commonly held beliefs, case studies, and analogies) directly supports explanations.	Evidence supports explanations but with little variety.	Little evidence supports explanations, or only one kind of evidence is used.	Supporting evidence is lacking.

WORKSHOP SCALES AND RUBRICS

Workshop Scales and Rubrics **87**

NAME _____ CLASS _____ DATE _____

for COLLECTION 10 continued

ANALYTICAL SCORING RUBRIC

CRITERIA FOR EVALUATION	SCORE POINT 4	SCORE POINT 3	SCORE POINT 2	SCORE POINT 1
Cause-effect clue words help explain the situation and its negative effects.	Cause-effect clue words help explain the situation and its negative effects and clearly link ideas.	Cause-effect clue words sometimes help explain the situation and its negative effects.	Few cause-effect clue words help explain the situation, or they are ambiguous.	Cause-effect clue words are scarce and/or are used inappropriately.
Conclusion addresses readers' counterclaims.	Conclusion convincingly addresses the readers' counterclaims.	Conclusion mentions, but does not respond to, the readers' counterclaims.	Conclusion only alludes to readers' counterclaims.	Counterclaims are not addressed.
Conclusion restates opinion statement.	Conclusion freshly restates opinion statement.	Conclusion restates opinion statement but is incomplete.	Opinion statement in conclusion is largely unrelated to information in essay.	Opinion statement is missing.
Conclusion includes a specific call to action and ends with a strong statement.	Conclusion includes a specific call to action necessary for making a change and ends with a strong statement.	Conclusion includes a specific call to action and ends with a pertinent, but not convincing, statement.	Conclusion includes a weak call to action or ends with a general statement.	Conclusion ends abruptly without a call to action or ending statement.

▶ **Language Conventions**

Standard English spelling, punctuation, capitalization, and manuscript form are used appropriately for this grade level.	Standard English spelling, punctuation, capitalization, and manuscript form are used appropriately for this grade level throughout the essay.	Standard English spelling, punctuation, capitalization, and manuscript form are used appropriately for this grade level, with few problems.	Inconsistent use of standard English spelling, punctuation, capitalization, and manuscript form disrupts readers' comprehension.	Minimal use of standard English spelling, punctuation, capitalization, and manuscript form confuses the readers.
Standard English sentence and paragraph structure, grammar, usage, and diction are used appropriately for this grade level.	Standard English sentence and paragraph structure, grammar, usage, and diction are used appropriately for this grade level throughout the essay.	Standard English sentence and paragraph structure, grammar, usage, and diction are used appropriately for this grade level, with few problems.	Inconsistent use of standard English sentence and paragraph structure, grammar, usage, and diction disrupts readers' comprehension.	Minimal use of standard English sentence and paragraph structure, grammar, usage, and diction confuses the readers.

NAME _____ CLASS _____ DATE _____

for **COLLECTION 10** *page 842*

ANALYTICAL SCALE

Speaking: Persuasive Speech

Use the chart below to evaluate a persuasive speech. Circle the numbers that best indicate how well the criteria are met. With these nine criteria, the lowest possible score is 0, the highest 36.

4 = Clearly meets this criterion
3 = Makes a serious effort to meet this criterion and is fairly successful
2 = Makes some effort to meet this criterion but with little success
1 = Does not achieve this criterion
0 = Unscorable

CRITERIA FOR EVALUATION	RATINGS
Content, Organization, and Delivery	
Introduction makes a dramatic impact with an intriguing literary quotation, an interesting anecdote, or a reference to an authority on the subject.	4 3 2 1
Information is relevant, valid, credible, and compelling to the audience.	4 3 2 1
Rhetorical devices—emotional, logical, and ethical appeals—suit the audience for effectiveness.	4 3 2 1
Concerns and counterclaims are anticipated and addressed.	4 3 2 1
Cause-effect clue words show order of ideas and make the relationship between causes and effects clear.	4 3 2 1
Conclusion summarizes effects of situation.	4 3 2 1
Conclusion restates opinion in a memorable fashion.	4 3 2 1
Verbal and nonverbal techniques emphasize particular points.	4 3 2 1
Language Conventions	
Standard English grammar, usage, and diction are used appropriately for this grade level.	4 3 2 1
Total Points:	

Workshop Scales and Rubrics **89**

NAME _____ CLASS _____ DATE _____

for COLLECTION 11 page 1040

ANALYTICAL SCALE

Writing: Comparing a Play and a Film

Use the chart below (and the rubric on pages 91–92) to evaluate a comparison of a play and a film. Circle the numbers that best indicate how well the criteria are met. With these nine criteria, the lowest possible score is 0, the highest 36.

4 = Clearly meets this criterion
3 = Makes a serious effort to meet this criterion and is fairly successful
2 = Makes some effort to meet this criterion but with little success
1 = Does not achieve this criterion
0 = Unscorable

CRITERIA FOR EVALUATION	RATINGS
Genre, Organization, and Focus	
An interesting opening engages readers immediately.	4 3 2 1
Original play and film and their creators are identified in first paragraph.	4 3 2 1
Thesis statement identifies the response the filmmaker was trying to create.	4 3 2 1
Evidence supports discussion of both narrative and film techniques.	4 3 2 1
Organization of ideas is easy to follow.	4 3 2 1
Conclusion restates thesis.	4 3 2 1
Essay ends with concluding thought or question.	4 3 2 1
Language Conventions	
Standard English spelling, punctuation, capitalization, and manuscript form are used appropriately for this grade level.	4 3 2 1
Standard English sentence and paragraph structure, grammar, usage, and diction (with emphasis on use of active voice) are used appropriately for this grade level.	4 3 2 1
Total Points:	

90   Holt Assessment: Writing, Listening, and Speaking

NAME _____ CLASS _____ DATE _____

for **COLLECTION 11** page 1040

ANALYTICAL SCORING RUBRIC

Writing: Comparing a Play and a Film

CRITERIA FOR EVALUATION	SCORE POINT 4	SCORE POINT 3	SCORE POINT 2	SCORE POINT 1
Genre, Organization, and Focus				
An interesting opening engages readers immediately.	An interesting opening engages readers immediately with a quotation from the play, an intriguing question, or a relevant anecdote.	The opening interests readers, but not immediately.	Opening is relevant but does not take readers into account.	Opening is uninteresting.
Original play and film and their creators are identified in first paragraph.	Original play and film and their creators are accurately identified in first paragraph.	Original play and film and their creators are incompletely identified in first paragraph.	Either original play, film version, or their creators are identified in essay.	Original play, film version, or their creators are not identified or are inaccurately named.
Thesis statement identifies the responses the filmmaker was trying to create.	Clear thesis statement identifies the intellectual or emotional responses the filmmaker was trying to create.	Thesis statement identifies the responses the filmmaker was trying to create but is not adequately specific.	Thesis statement is unclear or mistakenly identifies the responses the filmmaker was trying to create.	Thesis statement is missing.
Evidence supports discussion of both narrative and film techniques.	Specific references to the play and film support and elaborate on discussion of both narrative and film techniques.	General references to the play and film support discussion of both narrative and film techniques.	Evidence is sparse and supports discussion of only narrative or film techniques.	Evidence is missing or supports only a single technique.
Organization of ideas is easy to follow.	Organization of ideas is easy to follow, with narrative techniques in point-by-point order and film techniques in order of importance.	The organization of most ideas is easy to follow, with few breakdowns.	Disconnected ideas are difficult to follow.	Organization is confusing.
Conclusion restates thesis.	Conclusion clearly and freshly restates thesis.	Conclusion restates thesis in a repetitive manner.	Conclusion merely alludes to thesis.	No thesis or restatement is apparent.

WORKSHOP SCALES AND RUBRICS

Workshop Scales and Rubrics **91**

for **COLLECTION 11** continued

ANALYTICAL SCORING RUBRIC

CRITERIA FOR EVALUATION	SCORE POINT 4	SCORE POINT 3	SCORE POINT 2	SCORE POINT 1
Essay ends with concluding thought or question.	Essay ends with interesting concluding thought, question, or summary that leaves readers something to ponder.	Essay ends with concluding thought or question that is not particularly interesting.	Essay ends with concluding thought or question that is not pertinent to thesis.	Essay ends abruptly or rambles on.

Language Conventions

Standard English spelling, punctuation, capitalization, and manuscript form are used appropriately for this grade level.	Standard English spelling, punctuation, capitalization, and manuscript form are used appropriately for this grade level throughout the essay.	Standard English spelling, punctuation, capitalization, and manuscript form are used appropriately for this grade level, with few problems.	Inconsistent use of standard English spelling, punctuation, capitalization, and manuscript form disrupts readers' comprehension.	Minimal use of standard English spelling, punctuation, capitalization, and manuscript form confuses the readers.
Standard English sentence and paragraph structure, grammar, usage, and diction (with emphasis on use of active voice) are used appropriately for this grade level.	Standard English sentence and paragraph structure, grammar, usage, and diction (with emphasis on use of active voice) are used appropriately for this grade level throughout the essay.	Standard English sentence and paragraph structure, grammar, usage, and diction (with emphasis on use of active voice) are used appropriately for this grade level, with few problems.	Inconsistent use of standard English sentence and paragraph structure, grammar, usage, and diction disrupts readers' comprehension.	Minimal use of standard English sentence and paragraph structure, grammar, usage, and diction confuses the readers.

NAME _____ CLASS _____ DATE _____

for **COLLECTION 11** page 1048

ANALYTICAL SCALE

Listening: Analyzing and Evaluating Speeches

Use the chart below to assess students' evaluation of a historically significant speech. Circle the numbers that best indicate how well the criteria are met. For students who evaluate a recorded speech, use all five criteria. With these five criteria, the lowest possible score is 0, the highest 20. For students who evaluate a written speech, use only the first three criteria. With these three criteria, the lowest possible score is 0, the highest 12.

4 = Clearly meets this criterion
3 = Makes a serious effort to meet this criterion and is fairly successful
2 = Makes some effort to meet this criterion but with little success
1 = Does not achieve this criterion
0 = Unscorable

CRITERIA FOR EVALUATION	RATINGS
The Student	
Evaluates arguments (causation, analogies, appeals to authority, emotional and logical appeals) used by the speaker	4 3 2 1
Evaluates rhetorical devices (allusions, metaphor, repetition, diction, and parallelism) used by the speaker	4 3 2 1
Evaluates and describes the organizational pattern	4 3 2 1
Evaluates how the speaker uses verbal techniques (emphasis, pauses, and enunciation) to get points across to the audience	4 3 2 1
Evaluates how the speaker uses nonverbal techniques (gestures, facial expressions, and posture) to set the tone and mood	4 3 2 1
Total Points:	

WORKSHOP SCALES AND RUBRICS

Workshop Scales and Rubrics   **93**

NAME _____ CLASS _____ DATE _____

for **COLLECTION 12** page 1084

ANALYTICAL SCALE

Writing: Business Letter

Use the chart below to evaluate a business letter. Circle the numbers that best indicate how well the criteria are met. With these six criteria, the lowest possible score is 0, the highest 24.

4 = Clearly meets this criterion
3 = Makes a serious effort to meet this criterion and is fairly successful
2 = Makes some effort to meet this criterion but with little success
1 = Does not achieve this criterion
0 = Unscorable

CRITERIA FOR EVALUATION	RATINGS
Genre, Organization, and Focus	
Style and tone of letter are formal and respectful.	4 3 2 1
Central idea is clearly stated in first paragraph.	4 3 2 1
Letter clearly and briefly provides all the information the recipient of the letter needs to know.	4 3 2 1
Vocabulary is appropriate to the situation.	4 3 2 1
Proper block-style or modified-block-style format is used.	4 3 2 1
Language Conventions	
Standard English is used appropriately for this grade level.	4 3 2 1
Total Points:	

WORKSHOP SCALES AND RUBRICS

94 Holt Assessment: Writing, Listening, and Speaking

Scales and Sample Papers

Analytical Scale: 7 Writing Traits

IDEAS AND CONTENT

Score 5

The paper is clear, focused, and engaging. Its thoughtful, concrete details capture the reader's attention and flesh out the central theme, main idea, or story line.

- *A score "5" paper has the following characteristics.*
  - ✓ The topic is clearly focused and manageable for a paper of its kind; it is not overly broad or scattered.
  - ✓ Ideas are original and creative.
  - ✓ The writer appears to be working from personal knowledge or experience.
  - ✓ Key details are insightful and well considered; they are not obvious, predictable, or humdrum.
  - ✓ The development of the topic is thorough and purposeful; the writer anticipates and answers the reader's questions.
  - ✓ Supporting details are never superfluous or merely ornamental; every detail contributes to the whole.

Score 3

The writer develops the topic in a general or basic way; although clear, the paper remains routine or broad.

- *A score "3" paper has the following characteristics.*
  - ✓ Although the topic may be fuzzy, it is still possible to understand the writer's purpose and to predict how the paper will be developed.
  - ✓ Support is present, but somewhat vague and unhelpful in illustrating the key issues or main idea; the writer makes references to his or her own experience or knowledge, but has difficulty moving from general observations to specifics.
  - ✓ Ideas are understandable, yet not detailed, elaborated upon, or personalized; the writer's ideas do not reveal any deep comprehension of the topic or of the writing task.
  - ✓ The writer does not stray from the topic, but ideas remain general or slightly implicit; more information is necessary to fill in the gaps.

Score 1

The paper does not exhibit any clear purpose or main idea. The reader must use the scattered details to infer a coherent and meaningful message.

- *A score "1" paper has the following characteristics.*
  - ✓ The writer seems not to have truly settled on a topic; the essay reads like a series of brainstorming notes or disconnected, random thoughts.
  - ✓ The thesis is a vague statement of the topic rather than a main idea about the topic; in addition, there is little or no support or detail.
  - ✓ Information is very limited or vague; readers must make inferences to fill in gaps of logic or to identify any progression of ideas.
  - ✓ Text may be rambling and repetitious; alternatively, the length may not be adequate for a thoughtful development of ideas.
  - ✓ There is no subordination of ideas; every idea seems equally weighted or ideas are not tied to an overarching idea.

Analytical Scale: 7 Writing Traits (continued)

ORGANIZATION

Score 5

Organization enables the clear communication of the central idea or story line. The order of information draws the reader effortlessly through the text.

- *A score "5" paper has the following characteristics.*
  - ✓ The sequencing is logical and effective; ideas and details "fit" where the writer has placed them.
  - ✓ The essay contains an interesting or inviting introduction and a satisfying conclusion.
  - ✓ The pacing is carefully controlled; the writer slows down to provide explanation or elaboration when appropriate and increases the pace when necessary.
  - ✓ Transitions carefully connect ideas and cue the reader to specific relationships between ideas.
  - ✓ The choice of organizational structure is appropriate to the writer's purpose and audience.
  - ✓ If present, the title sums up the central idea of the paper in a fresh or thoughtful way.

Score 3

Organization is reasonably strong; it enables the reader to move continually forward without undue confusion.

- *A score "3" paper has the following characteristics.*
  - ✓ The essay has an introduction and conclusion. However, the introduction may not be inviting or engaging; the conclusion may not knit all the paper's ideas together with a summary or restatement.
  - ✓ Sequencing is logical but predictable. Sometimes, the sequence may be so formulaic that it detracts from the content.
  - ✓ At times, the sequence may not consistently support the essay's ideas; the reader may wish to reorder sections mentally or to supply transitions as he or she reads.
  - ✓ Pacing is reasonably well done, although sometimes the writer moves ahead too quickly or spends too much time on unimportant details.
  - ✓ At times, transitions may be fuzzy, showing unclear connections between ideas.
  - ✓ If present, the title may be dull or a simple restatement of the topic or prompt.

Score 1

Writing does not exhibit a sense of purpose or writing strategy. Ideas, details, or events appear to be cobbled together without any internal structure.

- *A score "1" paper has the following characteristics.*
  - ✓ Sequencing needs work; one idea or event does not logically follow another. Organizational problems make it difficult for the reader to understand the main idea.
  - ✓ There is no real introduction to guide the reader into the paper; neither is there any real conclusion or attempt to tie things up at the end.
  - ✓ Pacing is halting or inconsistent; the writer may slow the pace or speed up at inappropriate times.
  - ✓ Ideas are connected with confusing transitions; alternatively, connections are altogether absent.
  - ✓ If present, the title does not accurately reflect the content of the essay.

Analytical Scale: 7 Writing Traits (continued)

VOICE

Score 5

The writing is expressive and engaging. In addition, the writer seems to have a clear awareness of audience and purpose.

- *A score "5" paper has the following characteristics.*
  - ✓ The tone of the writing is appropriate for the purpose and audience of the paper.
  - ✓ The reader is aware of a real person behind the text; if appropriate, the writer takes risks in revealing a personal dimension throughout the piece.
  - ✓ If the paper is expository or persuasive, the writer shows a strong connection to the topic and explains why the reader should care about the issue.
  - ✓ If the paper is a narrative, the point of view is sincere, interesting, and compelling.

Score 3

The writer is reasonably genuine but does not reveal any excitement or connection with the issue. The resulting paper is pleasant but not truly engaging.

- *A score "3" paper has the following characteristics.*
  - ✓ The writer offers obvious generalities instead of personal insights.
  - ✓ The writer uses neutral language and a slightly flattened tone.
  - ✓ The writer communicates in an earnest and pleasing manner, yet takes no risks. In only a few instances is the reader captivated or moved.
  - ✓ Expository or persuasive writing does not reveal a consistent engagement with the topic; there is no attempt to build credibility with the audience.
  - ✓ Narrative writing doesn't reveal a fresh or individual perspective.

Score 1

Writing is mechanical or wooden. The writer appears indifferent to the topic and/or the audience.

- *A score "1" paper has the following characteristics.*
  - ✓ The writer shows no concern with the audience; the voice may be jarringly inappropriate for the intended reader.
  - ✓ The development of the topic is so limited that no identifiable point of view is present; or the writing is so short that it offers little but a general introduction of the topic.
  - ✓ The writer seems to speak in a monotone, using a voice that suppresses all excitement about the message.
  - ✓ Although the writing may communicate on a functional level, the writing is ordinary and takes no risks; depending on the topic, it may be overly technical or jargonistic.

Analytical Scale: 7 Writing Traits *(continued)*

WORD CHOICE

Score 5

Words are precise, engaging, and unaffected. They convey the writer's message in an interesting and effective way.

- *A score "5" paper has the following characteristics.*
  - ✓ All words are specific and appropriate. In all instances, the writer has taken care to choose the right words or phrases.
  - ✓ The paper's language is natural, not overwrought; it never shows a lack of control. Clichés and jargon are rarely used.
  - ✓ The paper contains energetic verbs; precise nouns and modifiers provide clarity.
  - ✓ The writer uses vivid words and phrases, including sensory details; such language creates distinct images in the reader's mind.

Score 3

Despite its lack of flair, the paper's language gets the message across. It is functional and clear.

- *A score "3" paper has the following characteristics.*
  - ✓ Words are correct and generally adequate, but lack originality or precision.
  - ✓ Familiar words and phrases do not pique the reader's interest or imagination. Lively verbs and phrases perk things up occasionally, but the paper does not consistently sparkle.
  - ✓ There are attempts at engaging or academic language, but they sometimes seem overly showy or pretentious.
  - ✓ The writing contains passive verbs and basic nouns and adjectives, and it lacks precise adverbs.

Score 1

The writer's limited vocabulary impedes communication; he or she seems to struggle for words to convey a clear message.

- *A score "1" paper has the following characteristics.*
  - ✓ Vague language communicates an imprecise or incomplete message. The reader is left confused or unsure of the writer's purpose.
  - ✓ Words are used incorrectly. In addition, frequent misuse of parts of speech impairs understanding.
  - ✓ Excessive redundancy in the paper is distracting.
  - ✓ The writing overuses jargon or clichés.

Analytical Scale: 7 Writing Traits *(continued)*

SENTENCE FLUENCY

Score 5

Sentences are thoughtfully constructed, and sentence structure is varied throughout the paper. When read aloud, the writing is fluent and rhythmic.

- *A score "5" paper has the following characteristics.*
  - ✓ The sentences are constructed so that meaning is clear to the reader.
  - ✓ Sentences vary in length and in structure.
  - ✓ Varied sentence beginnings add interest and clarity.
  - ✓ The writing has a steady beat; the reader is able to read the text effortlessly, without confusion or stumbling.
  - ✓ Dialogue, if used, is natural. Any fragments are used purposefully and contribute to the paper's style.
  - ✓ Thoughtful connectives and transitions between sentences reveal how the paper's ideas work together.

Score 3

The text maintains a steady rhythm, but the reader may find it more flat or mechanical than fluent or musical.

- *A score "3" paper has the following characteristics.*
  - ✓ Sentences are usually grammatical and unified, but they are routine rather than artful. The writer has not paid a great deal of attention to how the sentences sound.
  - ✓ There is some variation in sentence length and structure as well as in sentence beginnings. Not all sentences are constructed exactly the same way.
  - ✓ The reader may have to search for transitional words and phrases that show how sentences relate to one another. Sometimes, such context clues are entirely absent when they should be present.
  - ✓ Although sections of the paper invite expressive oral reading, the reader may also encounter many stilted or awkward sections.

Score 1

The reader will encounter challenges in reading the choppy or confusing text; meaning may be significantly obscured by the errors in sentence construction.

- *A score "1" paper has the following characteristics.*
  - ✓ The sentences do not "hang together." They are run-on, incomplete, monotonous, or awkward.
  - ✓ Phrasing often sounds too sing-song, not natural. The paper does not invite expressive oral reading.
  - ✓ Nearly all the sentences begin the same way, and they may all follow the same pattern (e.g., subject-verb-object). The result may be a monotonous repetition of sounds.
  - ✓ Endless connectives or a complete lack of connectives creates a confused muddle of language.

Analytical Scale: 7 Writing Traits *(continued)*

CONVENTIONS

Score 5

Standard writing conventions (e.g., spelling, punctuation, capitalization, grammar, usage, and paragraphing) are used correctly and in a way that aids the reader's understanding. Any errors tend to be minor; the piece is nearly ready for publication.

- *A score "5" paper has the following characteristics.*
  - ✓ Paragraphing is regular and enhances the organization of the paper.
  - ✓ Grammar and usage are correct and add clarity to the text as a whole. Sometimes, the writer may manipulate conventions in a controlled way—especially grammar and spelling—for stylistic effect.
  - ✓ Punctuation is accurate; it enables the reader to move through the text with understanding and ease.
  - ✓ The writer's understanding of capitalization rules is evident throughout the paper.
  - ✓ Most words, even difficult ones, are spelled correctly.

Score 3

The writer exhibits an awareness of a limited set of standard writing conventions and uses them to enhance the paper's readability. Although the writer shows control, at times errors distract the reader or impede communication. Moderate editing is required for publication.

- *A score "3" paper has the following characteristics.*
  - ✓ Paragraphs are used, but may begin in the wrong places, or sections that should be separate paragraphs are run together.
  - ✓ Conventions may not always be correct. However, problems with grammar and usage are usually not serious enough to distort meaning.
  - ✓ Terminal (end-of-sentence) punctuation is usually correct; internal punctuation (e.g., commas, apostrophes, semicolons, parentheses) may be missing or wrong.
  - ✓ Common words are usually spelled correctly.
  - ✓ Most words are capitalized correctly, but the writer's command of more sophisticated capitalization skills is inconsistent.

Score 1

There are errors in spelling, punctuation, usage and grammar, capitalization, and/or paragraphing that seriously impede the reader's comprehension. Extensive editing is required for publication.

- *A score "1" paper has the following characteristics.*
  - ✓ Paragraphing is missing, uneven, or too frequent. Most of the paragraphs do not reinforce or support the organizational structure of the paper.
  - ✓ Errors in grammar and usage are very common and distracting; such errors also affect the paper's meaning.
  - ✓ Punctuation, including terminal punctuation, is often missing or incorrect.
  - ✓ Even common words are frequently misspelled.
  - ✓ Capitalization is haphazard or reveals the writer's understanding of only the simplest rules.
  - ✓ The paper must be read once just to decode the language and then again to capture the paper's meaning.

Analytical Scale: 7 Writing Traits *(continued)*

PRESENTATION

Score 5

The presentation of the writing is clear and visually appealing. The format helps the reader focus on the message of the writing.

- *A score "5" paper has the following characteristics.*
  - ✓ If the paper is handwritten, all letters are formed clearly, and the slant and spacing are consistent.
  - ✓ If the paper is word processed, fonts and font sizes are appropriate for the genre of writing and assist the reader's comprehension.
  - ✓ White space and text are balanced.
  - ✓ Text markers, such as title, headings, and numbering, highlight important information and aid reading of the text.
  - ✓ If visuals are used, they are appropriate to the writing, are integrated effectively with the text, and clearly communicate and enhance the message.

Score 3

The presentation of the writing is readable and understandable; however, inconsistencies in format at times detract from the text.

- *A score "3" paper has the following characteristics.*
  - ✓ If the paper is handwritten, the handwriting is legible, but some inconsistencies occur in spacing and the formation and slant of letters.
  - ✓ If the paper is word processed, fonts and font sizes are inconsistent, sometimes distracting the reader.
  - ✓ White space and text are consistent, although a different use of space would make the paper easier to read.
  - ✓ Text markers, such as title, headings, and numbering, are used to some degree; however, they are inconsistent and only occasionally helpful to the reader.
  - ✓ Visuals are sometimes ineffective and not clearly linked to the text.

Score 1

The presentation and format of the writing are confusing, making the paper difficult to read and understand.

- *A score "1" paper has the following characteristics.*
  - ✓ If the paper is handwritten, the letters are formed incorrectly or irregularly. The inconsistent slant and spacing make the paper difficult to read.
  - ✓ If the paper is word processed, fonts and font sizes are used randomly or inappropriately, disrupting the reader's comprehension.
  - ✓ Spacing appears random, with use of white space either excessive or minimal.
  - ✓ Text markers, such as title, headings, and numbering, are not used.
  - ✓ Visuals are inaccurate, inappropriate, misleading, or confusing.

Biographical or Autobiographical Narrative Holistic Scale

Score 4

This distinctly purposeful narrative has an engaging and meaningful introduction, presents a logical sequence of events, and relies on concrete sensory details. The significance of the events is clearly communicated.

- **The writing strongly demonstrates**
  - ✓ thorough attention to all parts of the writing task
  - ✓ a strong and meaningful purpose, consistent tone and focus, and thoughtfully effective organization
  - ✓ a distinct understanding of audience
  - ✓ great proficiency in relating a sequence of events and their significance to the audience
  - ✓ consistent use of concrete sensory details to describe the sights, sounds, and smells of a scene
  - ✓ variation of sentence types using precise, descriptive language
  - ✓ a solid command of English-language conventions. Errors, if any, are minor and unobtrusive.

Score 3

This purposeful narrative has a meaningful introduction, presents a logical sequence of events, and clearly communicates the significance of those events.

- **The writing generally demonstrates**
  - ✓ attention to all parts of the writing task
  - ✓ clear purpose, a consistent tone and focus, and effective organization
  - ✓ an understanding of audience
  - ✓ an ability to relate a sequence of events and their significance to the audience
  - ✓ frequent use of concrete sensory details to describe the sights, sounds, and smells of a scene
  - ✓ variation of sentence types using some descriptive language
  - ✓ a command of English-language conventions. Few errors exist, and they do not interfere with the reader's understanding of the narrative.

Score 2

This narrative has a somewhat vague introduction. The sequence or significance of the events is unclear.

- **The writing demonstrates**
  - ✓ attention to only parts of the writing task
  - ✓ vague purpose, an inconsistent tone and focus, and less than effective organization
  - ✓ little or no understanding of audience
  - ✓ a weak ability to relate a sequence of events and their significance to the audience
  - ✓ infrequent use of concrete sensory details to describe the sights, sounds, and smells of a scene
  - ✓ little variation in sentence type; use of basic, predictable descriptive language
  - ✓ inconsistent use of English-language conventions. Errors may interfere with the reader's understanding of the narrative.

Biographical or Autobiographical Narrative Holistic Scale *(continued)*

Score 1

This narrative has a vague introduction and displays no clear purpose. Events are disorganized and their significance is hidden.

- *The writing lacks*
  ✓ attention to most parts of the writing task
  ✓ a purpose (or provides only a weak sense of purpose), a focus, and effective organization
  ✓ an understanding of audience
  ✓ proficiency in relating a sequence of events to the audience
  ✓ concrete sensory details to describe the sights, sounds, and smells of a scene
  ✓ sentence variety and descriptive vocabulary
  ✓ a basic understanding of English-language conventions. Numerous errors often interfere with the reader's understanding of the narrative.

STUDENT MODEL

Autobiographical Narrative: Sample A

> **PROMPT**
>
> Think about a special time that you spent with your family or friends. What made your time together significant? Write a well-developed autobiographical narrative about this special time, relating a sequence of events and their significance. Remember to use concrete sensory details to describe the events.

Like magic carpet rides, my mother's stories instantly transported me to distant times and places. My mother, Carlotta Maria Paloma Chavez, was born and raised on the Texas plains. As a child, she loved the way she could see for great distances. Only now and then would a tree pierce the sky, breaking the limitless horizon. "Otherwise," she would say, "you could see forever." She called it "seeing the long view."

Every now and then, when life became too hard or lonely, my mother would look at me and say, "Let's go see the long view." Then the two of us would take off for the afternoon and ride the Staten Island Ferry. Once on the boat, we were no longer alone or weary. Sometimes as we rode the ferry, my mother talked about her life in Texas. For a few hours at least, the ferry was a place where we forgot our problems among the fresh smells of the sea, the harsh calls of the gulls, and the brisk breeze in our hair. The long views, out on the water, were soothing.

The cost of the ride matched our pocketbooks. There's an old saying that you get what you pay for. In the case of the Staten Island Ferry, we got much more. The cost of the ferry has always been low, but since July 4, 1997, the ride has been free.

Few other places can bring back the sheer pleasure that my mother and I experienced on our ferry rides. The trip from Manhattan to Staten Island gave us a fresh, new outlook on life. Seeing the beautiful skyline of lower Manhattan and the valiant figure of the Statue of Liberty made us forget the petty things that had been

Autobiographical Narrative: Sample A *(continued)*

wearing us down. The ride worked its same magic on the big problems, the ones that sometimes felt too overwhelming to solve. Those rides let us rediscover what was important to us.

Now I know what my mother was trying to teach me. When life's worries become too big a burden, it's time to slow down, put things in perspective, and see the long view.

FOR THE TEACHER

SCORING

Autobiographical Narrative: Sample A Evaluation

Holistic Scale

Rating: 4 points

Note: This essay illustrates the type of development appropriate for the prompt, but some teachers may ask their students to write longer essays.

Comments: This autobiographical narrative is colorful and well written. The introduction includes a simile, "Like magic carpet rides …," that grabs the reader's attention. The essay's purpose is distinct and meaningful, and concrete sensory details describe the sights, sounds, and smells of the ferry ride. Events are presented in a logical order, and their significance is clearly communicated. Tone and focus are consistent. Sentences are varied and use precise descriptive details. The narrative shows a solid command of English-language conventions.

Analytical Scale: 6 Traits—Plus 1

Ratings (High score is 5.)
Ideas and Content: 5   Sentence Fluency: 4
Organization: 5   Conventions: 5
Voice: 5   Presentation: 4
Word Choice: 4

Comments:

Ideas and Content: The topic is focused and thoroughly developed, and the essay relies on personal knowledge and original ideas as it relates the narrative. Well-considered supporting details help the reader visualize the scene and help convey the events' significance.

Organization: The narrative has an interesting introduction and satisfying conclusion. The sequence of events is logical. Effective transitions help connect ideas and cue the reader to relationships between ideas.

Voice: The tone is appropriate for an autobiographical narrative. A personal dimension is revealed throughout the essay, and the voice is sincere and compelling.

Word Choice: The narrative's language is natural. Vivid sensory details help create distinct images in the reader's mind. Words are specific and appropriate.

Sentence Fluency: Sentences are varied in length and structure, and they are clear. The text can be read with little effort. Transitions help reveal how the narrative's ideas work together. Dialogue is used naturally and purposefully.

Conventions: Effective paragraphing enhances the essay's organization, and the writer demonstrates a strong command of English-language conventions.

Presentation: The presentation is simple and clear.

108 Holt Assessment: Writing, Listening, and Speaking

STUDENT MODEL

Autobiographical Narrative: Sample B

PROMPT

Think about a special time that you spent with your family or friends. What made your time together significant? Write a well-developed autobiographical narrative about this special time, relating a sequence of events and their significance. Remember to use concrete sensory details to describe the events.

Like magic carpet rides, my mother's stories took me to other places. My mother, Carlotta Maria Paloma Chavez, was born and raised on the Texas Plains. I know that as a child she liked the way she could see for great distances. Only now and then was there a tree on the horizon. "Otherwise" she would say "you could see forever." She called it "seeing the long view."

Sometimes when life became too hard or lonly, my mother would look at me and say "let's go see the long view." The two of us would take off for the afternoon and take the Staten Island Ferry. My mother would talk about her life in Texas. The ferry was a place where we forgot our problems among the smells of the sea, the calls of the gulls, and the breeze in our hair. The long views were soothing.

The cost of the ride matched our pocketbooks. There's an old saying that you get what you pay for. In the case of the Staten Island Ferry, we got much more.

Few other places can bring back the sheer pleasure that my mother and I experienced on our ferry rides. The trip from Manhattan to Staten island gave us a new outlook on life. Seeing the skyline of lower Manhattan and the Statue of Liberty made us forget the things that were bothering us. The ride worked its same magic on the big problems, the ones that sometimes felt too overwhelming to solve. Those rides let us rediscover what was important to us.

FOR THE TEACHER

SCORING

Autobiographical Narrative: Sample B Evaluation

Holistic Scale

Rating: 3 points

Comments: This autobiographical narrative is clear and well organized. The introduction includes a simile, "Like magic carpet rides …," that grabs the reader's attention. The purpose is clear, and some concrete sensory details describe the ferry ride. Events are presented in a logical order, and their significance is communicated clearly. Tone and focus are consistent. Most sentences are varied and clear, although more concrete details would improve the narrative. The narrative shows a good command of English-language conventions, though some errors exist, especially in punctuating dialogue.

Analytical Scale: 7 Writing Traits

Ratings (High score is 5.)
Ideas and Content: 3   Sentence Fluency: 3
Organization: 4   Conventions: 3
Voice: 3   Presentation: 4
Word Choice: 3

Comments:

Ideas and Content: The topic and purpose are clear. To make ideas more explicit, supporting details could be more specific and vivid.

Organization: The narrative has an interesting and original introduction. The sequence of events is logical. Transitions are needed to help connect ideas and cue the reader to relationships between ideas.

Voice: The tone is sometimes flat, begging for greater expression of feelings. The point of view is sincere, but obvious generalities should be replaced with specific personal insights.

Word Choice: Words are used correctly, but they lack originality and precision. Livelier verbs and phrases are needed.

Sentence Fluency: Most sentences are varied in length and structure but often are routine. Transitions are needed to help reveal how the narrative's ideas work together.

Conventions: The writer demonstrates a general command of English-language conventions. Some spelling errors exist, and there are errors in internal punctuation, especially with dialogue.

Presentation: The presentation is simple and clear.

Holt Assessment: Writing, Listening, and Speaking

Autobiographical Narrative: Sample C

STUDENT MODEL

> **PROMPT**
>
> Think about a special time that you spent with your family or friends. What made your time together significant? Write a well-developed autobiographical narrative about this special time, relating a sequence of events and their significance. Remember to use concrete sensory details to describe the events.

My mothers story's helped me picture other places. Carlotta Maria Paloma Chavez was borned and raised on the Texas Planes where it's flat as a pancake. She loved the way she could see a long ways. She called it "seeing the long view" Their is an old saying you get what you pay for. In the case of the Statton Island ferry we got a lot.

Every now and then my mother looked at me and would say "let's go see the long view." We took off for the afternoon to ride the Statton island ferry, sometimes my mother talked about her life in Texas. The ferry was a place where we forgot our problems, and the long views were soothing.

The trip from Manhattan to Statton island gave us a new outlook on life. Seeing the skyline and the Statue of Liberty made us forget things. Those rides let us rediscover what was important to us and made things clear as a bell.

FOR THE TEACHER

SCORING

Autobiographical Narrative: Sample C Evaluation

Holistic Scale

Rating: 2 points

Comments: The narrative displays an understanding of only part of the writing task. A purpose is implicit, but the tone is inconsistent, and the focus sometimes drifts. Very few concrete sensory details are used. Sentences are basic and unvaried in construction. The sequence of events is occasionally unclear, as is the significance of the events. Several errors in grammar, punctuation, and spelling interfere with the reader's understanding of parts of the narrative.

Analytical Scale: 7 Writing Traits

Ratings (High score is 5.)
Ideas and Content: 2	Sentence Fluency: 2
Organization: 1	Conventions: 2
Voice: 2	Presentation: 4
Word Choice: 2	

Comments:

Ideas and Content: The focus and purpose are unclear. The narrative lacks supporting details. Information is vague, forcing the reader to make inferences to fill in the gaps.

Organization: The narrative lacks a coherent introduction, and its conclusion abruptly appears. Ideas do not flow logically, suggesting a need for transitions and greater focus on the main idea.

Voice: Because the topic is underdeveloped, the point of view is not clearly identifiable. The writing is monotonous and takes few risks.

Word Choice: The language is vague and lacks originality. Clichés are overused and inappropriate.

Sentence Fluency: Sentences are monotonous and do not flow logically. Transitions are needed to improve clarity and readability. Nearly all sentences follow the same pattern, causing choppy, awkward reading.

Conventions: Serious errors in grammar, spelling, and punctuation are distracting and sometimes impede understanding.

Presentation: The presentation is clear.

Exposition: Holistic Scale

Score 4

This expository writing presents a clear thesis or controlling impression and supports it with precise, relevant evidence.

- *The writing strongly demonstrates*
  - ✓ a clear understanding of all parts of the writing task
  - ✓ a meaningful thesis or controlling impression, a consistent tone and focus, and a purposeful control of organization
  - ✓ use of specific details and examples to support the main ideas
  - ✓ a variety of sentence types using precise, descriptive language
  - ✓ a clear understanding of audience
  - ✓ inclusion of accurate information from all relevant perspectives
  - ✓ anticipation of and thorough attention to readers' possible misunderstandings, biases, and expectations
  - ✓ a solid command of English-language conventions. Errors, if any, are generally minor and unobtrusive.

Score 3

This expository writing presents a thesis or controlling impression and supports it with evidence.

- *The writing generally demonstrates*
  - ✓ an understanding of all parts of the writing task
  - ✓ a thesis or controlling impression, a consistent tone and focus, and a control of organization
  - ✓ use of details and examples to support the main ideas
  - ✓ a variety of sentence types using some descriptive language
  - ✓ an understanding of audience
  - ✓ inclusion of accurate information from relevant perspectives
  - ✓ anticipation of and attention to readers' possible misunderstandings, biases, and expectations
  - ✓ an understanding of English-language conventions. Some errors exist, but they do not interfere with the reader's understanding.

Score 2

This expository writing presents a thesis or controlling impression, but the thesis is not sufficiently supported.

- *The writing demonstrates*
  - ✓ an understanding of only parts of the writing task
  - ✓ a thesis or controlling impression (though not always); an inconsistent tone and focus; and little, if any, control of organization
  - ✓ use of limited, if any, details and examples to support the main ideas
  - ✓ little variation in sentence types; use of basic, predictable language
  - ✓ little or no understanding of audience
  - ✓ little or no inclusion of information from relevant perspectives

Scales and Sample Papers

Exposition: Holistic Scale *(continued)*

✓ little, if any, anticipation of and attention to readers' possible misunderstandings, biases, and expectations
✓ inconsistent use of English-language conventions. Several errors exist and may interfere with the reader's understanding.

Score 1

This expository writing may present a thesis or controlling impression, but it is not supported.

- *The writing lacks*

  ✓ an understanding of the writing task, addressing only one part
  ✓ a thesis or controlling impression (or provides only a weak one), a focus, and control of organization
  ✓ details and examples to support ideas
  ✓ sentence variety and adequate vocabulary
  ✓ an understanding of audience
  ✓ accurate information from relevant perspectives
  ✓ anticipation of and attention to readers' possible misunderstandings, biases, and expectations
  ✓ an understanding of English-language conventions. Serious errors interfere with the reader's understanding.

Exposition: Sample A

STUDENT MODEL

PROMPT

Think of a place that is important to you. Write a description of the place so that your reader can visualize it from what you write. Be sure that your concrete details point to the controlling impression. Explain why the place is important.

Almost everybody who has ever been in my room hates it. My friends cannot believe how I manage to pack so much stuff into such a small space, and my parents can't stand the clutter. To me, it's perfect — full of the things I like, arranged the way I like them.

As I walk through the doorway, the first thing I see is a low, rectangular shape against the window facing me. That's my bed, but you might not know it because it's covered with all my personal stuff, like clothes, sports equipment, books, magazines, and CDs. Lancelot, my golden retriever, spends a lot of time sprawled out on my bed. His favorite spot is next to my pillows.

On my left, I see my wooden dresser, which has a huge chip in the right front leg. That's where my friend Bobby kicked it by accident while he and I were practicing soccer moves one day. If I squint, the shape of the chip looks like a smiling goalie.

On top of the dresser is my CD player. I always listen to classical music in my room because that's what I like to play. When the kettledrums rumble, I feel a vibration in my stomach, as if the percussionist were right in the room with me.

Also on top of my dresser are a lot of fresh apples, oranges, and bananas in a big bowl. When I'm hungry, I just reach for one of my favorite fruits. Somehow, having appetizing food there makes my room seem like the place that has everything I need.

On my right, I see my desk. It's orderly, unlike the rest of the room and me! Looking at the tidy arrangement, I feel in control of my life. Books, pens, and paper are laid out in neat piles next to my new computer. My desk is a miniature futuristic city where the buildings are made out of school supplies.

Exposition: Sample A (continued)

Everything in my room is just the way I like it. It's not tidy, but it's my own retreat. If you cannot stand the sight of dirty socks on the floor or the smell of a freshly peeled banana, then my room is no place for you. However, it's perfect for Lancelot and me.

Exposition: Sample A Evaluation

FOR THE TEACHER

SCORING

Holistic Scale

Rating: 4 points

Note: This essay illustrates the type of development appropriate for the prompt, but some teachers may ask their students to write longer essays.

Comments: This is a well-written and well-organized essay. The introduction grabs the reader's attention by presenting a topic that many readers can understand. The controlling impression is clear and is supported by colorful, descriptive details. The informal tone is consistent and appropriate for the intended audience. Readers' potential biases, such as a bias against having food in the room, are anticipated and addressed. The writer uses a somewhat whimsical tone to address friends about a comical topic. Sentences are varied and clear, and English-language conventions are strictly observed.

Analytical Scale: 7 Writing Traits

Ratings (High score is 5.)
Ideas and Content: 5
Organization: 5
Voice: 4
Word Choice: 4
Sentence Fluency: 5
Conventions: 5
Presentation: 4

Comments:

Ideas and Content: The topic is well focused, and the writer uses personal knowledge and original ideas to relate the description. Potential reader biases are anticipated and addressed.

Organization: The essay is well organized, with an interesting introduction leading to a logical sequence of descriptive details.

Voice: The informal tone is used consistently in the paper and is appropriate for the audience.

Word Choice: The writer uses simple, direct, and precise wording to relate details.

Sentence Fluency: The writing is easy to read. Sentence beginnings are varied and interesting, and thoughtful transitions facilitate the logical flow of ideas.

Conventions: The writer demonstrates a strong command of English-language conventions.

Presentation: The presentation is simple and clear.

Exposition: Sample B

STUDENT MODEL

> **PROMPT**
>
> Think of a place that is important to you. Write a description of the place so that your reader can visualize it from what you write. Be sure that your concrete details point to the controlling impression. Explain why the place is important.

Almost everybody who has ever been in my room hates it. My friends cannot believe how I manage to pack so much stuff into such a small space and my parents can't stand the clutter.

The first thing you notice in my room is a low object against the window. That's my bed, but you might not know it because its covered with all my personal stuff. My dog spends a lot of time sprawled out on my bed.

My dresser, which has a huge chip in the right front leg is on my left. That's where my friend Bobby kicked it by accident while me and him were practicing soccer moves one day.

On top of the dresser is my CD player. I always listen to classycal music in my room because thats what I like to play. There are also a lot of fresh apples, oranges, and bananas in a bowl. When I'm hungry I just reach for one of my favorite fruits.

My desk is orderly, unlike the rest of the room and me. Looking at the neat arrangement, I feel in control of my life. Books, pens, and paper are laid out in neat piles next to my new computer.

Everything in my room is just the way I like it. It's messy, but it's my own retreat. If you don't like dirty socks on the floor or the smell of a banana, then my room is no place for you. But it's perfect for me and my dog.

FOR THE TEACHER

SCORING

Exposition: Sample B Evaluation

Holistic Scale

Rating: 3 points

Comments: The controlling impression is clear and is supported by details. Sentence types are varied. The reader's expected bias against untidiness is addressed by conceding the point rather than refuting it. The writing shows an understanding of English-language conventions, though some errors exist in punctuation, spelling, and grammar.

Analytical Scale: 7 Writing Traits

Ratings (High score is 5.)

Ideas and Content: 4	Sentence Fluency: 3
Organization: 3	Conventions: 3
Voice: 3	Presentation: 4
Word Choice: 3	

Comments:

Ideas and Content: The thesis is clear and supported. Support is underdeveloped, needing more concrete sensory details.

Organization: Basic organization is clear, although main details are not adequately elaborated.

Voice: The tone is appropriate for the audience but lacks flair. The reader is rarely engaged by lively descriptions.

Word Choice: Word choice is simple and clear. More specific adjectives would help the reader visualize the room.

Sentence Fluency: Most sentences are varied in length, but better transitions would improve clarity and flow.

Conventions: The essay contains errors in punctuation, spelling, and grammar, but the errors do not interfere with understanding.

Presentation: The presentation is clear.

Exposition: Sample C

STUDENT MODEL

> **PROMPT**
>
> Think of a place that is important to you. Write a description of the place so that your reader can visualize it from what you write. Be sure that your concrete details point to the controlling impression. Explain why the place is important.

Almost everbody in my room hates it. My friends cant believe how I can fit so much stuff in such a small room.

There is a low object against the window. That's my bed but you might not know it because its covered with all my stuff. My dog spends a lot of time sprawled out on my bed.

My dresser has a huge chip in the right front leg on my left. My friend Bobby kicked it by accident while we was practising soccer moves one day.

My CD player is on top of it. I always listen to classycal music in my room because thats what I like to play. There are apples, oranges, and bananas in a bowl. When I'm hungry I eat like a horse.

My desk is neat, but the rest of the room and me isn't. I'm in control when I look at my desk. My books, pens, and paper are in piles next to my computer.

My room is just the way I like it. Some people might think its messy but its just the way I like it.

FOR THE TEACHER

SCORING

Exposition: Sample C Evaluation

Holistic Scale

Rating: 2 points
Comments: The writer does not understand the writing task. Details do not contribute to a controlling impression. Paragraphs are run together or break at illogical points in the text, and there is little variety in sentence structure. Serious errors exist in grammar, punctuation, and spelling.

Analytical Scale: 7 Writing Traits

Ratings (High score is 5.)
Ideas and Content: 2   Sentence Fluency: 2
Organization: 2   Conventions: 2
Voice: 2   Presentation: 4
Word Choice: 2

Comments:
Ideas and Content: The controlling impression is vague and unsupported.
Organization: Paragraphs are poorly structured. The writing lacks transitions and a strong conclusion.
Voice: The tone is flat and shows little consideration of audience. The writing is too short to cover the topic.
Word Choice: The language is vague, and the writing contains the cliché "eat like a horse."
Sentence Fluency: Sentences are monotonous and do not flow logically. Nearly all sentences follow the same pattern, causing choppy, awkward reading.
Conventions: Serious errors in grammar, spelling, and punctuation are distracting.
Presentation: The presentation is clear.

Response to Literature: Holistic Scale

Score 4

This insightful response to literature presents a thoroughly supported thesis and illustrates a comprehensive grasp of the text and the author's use of literary devices.

- *The writing strongly demonstrates*
  - ✓ a thoughtful, comprehensive understanding of the text
  - ✓ support of the thesis and main ideas with specific textual details and examples that are accurate and coherent
  - ✓ a thorough understanding of the text's ambiguities, nuances, and complexities
  - ✓ a variety of sentence types using precise, descriptive language
  - ✓ a clear understanding of the author's use of literary and stylistic devices
  - ✓ a solid command of English-language conventions. Errors, if any, are generally minor and unobtrusive.

Score 3

This response to literature presents a clear thesis that is supported by details and examples.

- *The writing generally demonstrates*
  - ✓ a comprehensive understanding of the text
  - ✓ support of the thesis and main ideas with general textual details and examples that are accurate and coherent
  - ✓ an understanding of the text's ambiguities, nuances, and complexities
  - ✓ a variety of sentence types using some descriptive language
  - ✓ an understanding of the author's use of literary and stylistic devices
  - ✓ an understanding of English-language conventions. Some errors exist, but they do not interfere with the reader's understanding of the essay.

Score 2

This literary response presents a thesis, but it is not sufficiently supported. The writing shows little understanding of the text.

- *The writing demonstrates*
  - ✓ a limited understanding of the text
  - ✓ little, if any, support of the thesis and main ideas with textual details and examples
  - ✓ limited, or no, understanding of the text's ambiguities, nuances, and complexities
  - ✓ little variety in sentence types; use of basic, predictable language
  - ✓ a limited understanding of the author's use of literary and stylistic devices
  - ✓ inconsistent use of English-language conventions. Several errors exist and may interfere with the reader's understanding of the essay.

Response to Literature: Holistic Scale *(continued)*

Score 1

This literary response contains serious analytical and English-language errors. It shows no understanding of the text or of the author's use of literary devices.

- *The writing lacks*
  - ✓ a comprehensive understanding of the text
  - ✓ textual details and examples to support the thesis and main ideas
  - ✓ an understanding of the text's ambiguities, nuances, and complexities
  - ✓ sentence variety and adequate vocabulary
  - ✓ an understanding of the author's use of literary and stylistic devices
  - ✓ an understanding of English-language conventions. Serious errors interfere with the reader's understanding of the essay.

Response to Literature: Sample A

STUDENT MODEL

> **PROMPT**
>
> You have an interest in science, especially in the space program. You decide to read a biography of someone who has worked in the space program and write an analysis of the biography to share with your science teacher. Remember to support your thesis with details and examples.

In *Mae Jemison: A Space Biography*, the author, Della A. Yannuzzi, portrays Jemison as an extraordinary woman whose quest for personal achievement has led her to success in several different fields. Mae Jemison is the first African American woman astronaut, but that is only part of her remarkable life.

Yannuzzi suggests that the setting in which Jemison grew up helped nurture her talents. Her parents, Charlie and Dorothy Green Jemison, valued education highly. In 1959, when Mae was three, they moved the family from Decatur, Alabama, to Chicago, Illinois. They wanted to make sure that their three children received a better education than the segregated schools of the South offered African Americans. Jemison's parents encouraged her interest in science, which was then considered a nontraditional career choice for women—particularly women of color. Yannuzzi recounts how, when Jemison told her kindergarten teacher that she wanted to be a scientist when she grew up, the teacher responded, "You mean a nurse, don't you?" Nevertheless, at home she was allowed the freedom to pursue her natural interests and to think for herself.

Certain character traits were important factors in her success. Jemison's determination propelled her toward significant achievements. She became even more fascinated with science as she grew older. She avidly studied books on astronomy and science fiction and closely followed developments in the space program. The author demonstrates that Jemison learned to shape outcomes rather than wait for them to happen. Once, for a science fair project, she contacted a local hospital for information on sickle cell anemia. Before long, she had a part-time job in the hospital's lab, supplementing her science courses with practical experience. After winning a National

Response to Literature: Sample A (continued)

Achievement Scholarship, she went on to Stanford University, where she took courses in chemical engineering and in African and African American studies. Studying both these subjects showed her determination to learn about diverse fields.

Various milestone events and accomplishments began to fall into place. Jemison was drawn to the astronaut training program, but she realized that she was not fully qualified. To strengthen her credentials, she earned a degree in medicine from Cornell University and worked as a doctor, first in Los Angeles, and then with the Peace Corps, in Liberia and Sierra Leone. Since her historic 1992 flight aboard the space shuttle <u>Endeavour,</u> she has taught at Dartmouth College, promoted science education, and operated her own science and technology consulting firm.

Yannuzzi believes that for Jemison, "The future is still wide open as she continues to follow her dreams." Raised in a supportive family and determined to reach her goals, Jemison has fashioned a life of challenging and rewarding events and service. <u>Mae Jemison: A Space Biography</u> shows Jemison as an ambitious woman whose accomplishments go well beyond her role as an astronaut.

FOR THE TEACHER

SCORING

Response to Literature: Sample A Evaluation

Holistic Scale

Rating: 4 points

Note: This essay illustrates the type of development appropriate for the prompt, but some teachers may ask their students to write longer essays.

Comments: The literary response presents a well-defined thesis that is supported by interesting and relevant examples. The accurate citations of Jemison's academic credentials and varied professional career lend validity to the thesis. Sentence types are varied and use precise, descriptive language. The writing shows an excellent command of English-language fundamentals.

Analytical Scale: 7 Writing Traits

Ratings (High score is 5.)
Ideas and Content: 5
Organization: 4
Voice: 5
Word Choice: 5
Sentence Fluency: 5
Conventions: 5
Presentation: 4

Comments:

Ideas and Content: The thesis is well supported. The writing demonstrates a deep and thoughtful understanding of the text.

Organization: The introduction draws the reader into the analysis by citing Jemison's extraordinary achievement. Logical organization leads to a concise summary in the conclusion.

Voice: The tone reveals the writer's fascination with the topic.

Word Choice: Word choice is precise.

Sentence Fluency: Sentences are varied and well constructed.

Conventions: The writing shows an excellent command of grammar, usage, and mechanics.

Presentation: The presentation is simple and clear.

SCALES AND SAMPLE PAPERS

STUDENT MODEL

Response to Literature: Sample B

PROMPT

You have an interest in science, especially in the space program. You decide to read a biography of someone who has worked in the space program and write an analysis of the biography to share with your science teacher. Remember to support your thesis with details and examples.

In *Mae Jemison: A Space Biography*, the author Della A. Yannuzzi portrays Jemison as a special woman whose determination has led her to success. Mae Jemison is the first African American woman astronaut.

Yannuzzi says Jemison's childhood was important. Her parents Charlie and Dorothy Green Jemison valued education. In 1959 when Mae was three, they moved to Chicago, Illinois. Mae's parents encouraged her interest in science, which was considered a field mostly for men. Yannuzzi recounts how, when Mae told her kindergarten teacher that she wanted to be a scientist when she grew up, the teacher responded "you mean a nurse, don't you?". Mae became more interested in science as she grew older. She read books on Astronomy and Science Fiction and closely followed developments in the space program. By the time she was in high school, Yannuzzi explains, she was "Creating opportunities for herself".

After winning a National Achievement Scholarship, she went to Stanford University, where she earned a bachelor of science degree in Chemical Engineering and took courses in African and African American studies. To strengthen her credentials, she earned a degree in Medicine from Cornell University and worked as a doctor.

Jemison's determination really paid off after college. Since her historic 1992 flight aboard the Space Shuttle Endeavour, she has taught at Dartmouth College, promoted science education, and operated her own science and technology consulting firm.

Scales and Sample Papers

Response to Literature: Sample B (continued)

Yannuzzi believes that Jemison will continue to explore new challenges in the years to come. Jemison's determination, supportive home life, and education have led to a richly rewarding and varied life. <u>Mae Jemison: A Space Biography</u>, shows Jemison as someone who has succeeded in many areas.

FOR THE TEACHER

SCORING

Response to Literature: Sample B Evaluation

Holistic Scale

Rating: 3 points
Comments: The thesis is clear and is supported by an explanation of the elements of the biography. Sentence types are varied, but transitions and more precise language would help readability. The writing shows an understanding of English-language fundamentals, though some errors exist in punctuation and capitalization.

Analytical Scale: 7 Writing Traits

Ratings (High score is 5.)

Ideas and Content: 4	Sentence Fluency: 3
Organization: 3	Conventions: 3
Voice: 3	Presentation: 4
Word Choice: 3	

Comments:
Ideas and Content: The thesis is well focused, but more details and examples are needed to support the thesis and make the analysis more interesting.
Organization: Organization is not as clear as Sample A's. A more engaging opening would help grab the reader's interest, and transitions are needed to improve the flow of the text.
Voice: The tone is appropriate but remains somewhat flat, with neutral language and obvious generalities.
Word Choice: Word choice is correct and free of jargon, but general, commonplace nouns and adjectives could be replaced by more precise, descriptive words.
Sentence Fluency: Sentences are varied in length, but better transitions are needed.
Conventions: The essay contains some errors in punctuation and capitalization, but spelling is consistently correct.
Presentation: The presentation is clear.

Response to Literature: Sample C

STUDENT MODEL

> **PROMPT**
>
> You have an interest in science, especially in the space program. You decide to read a biography of someone who has worked in the space program and write an analysis of the biography to share with your science teacher. Remember to support your thesis with details and examples.

In *Mae Jemison: A Space Biography* the author displays Jemison as a successful women. Mae Jamison is the first African American woman who was an astronaut.

Her parents Charlie and Dorothy Green Jemison valued education. In 1959 they moved to Chicago, Illinois. Maes' parents encouraged her interest in science. It was considered a field mostly for men. Mae became more interested in science as she grew older. She red lots of sience books.

Jemison's hard work payed off after college, she flew on the space-shuttle Endeavor in 1992. She taught at Dartmouth college, promoted science education, and operated her own science and technology consulting firm (35).

Yannuzzi believes that Jemison will continue to explore new challenges in the years to come. Her determination, her parents, and her education led her to a really interesting and fun life. In the book, A Space Biography, Yanuzzi shows Jamison as someone who has done much more than just be an astronout.

Response to Literature: Sample C Evaluation

SCORING

FOR THE TEACHER

Holistic Scale

Rating: 2 points
Comments: The thesis, while understandable, is poorly worded and lacks insight. Supporting evidence is inadequate, and its relevance is sometimes unclear. Sentence structure is monotonous and in some cases nearly incomprehensible. Serious errors in punctuation and spelling impede readability. This literary response is far too short to address the complexities of the biography.

Analytical Scale: 7 Writing Traits

Ratings (High score is 5.)
Ideas and Content: 2
Organization: 3
Voice: 2
Word Choice: 2
Sentence Fluency: 2
Conventions: 2
Presentation: 3

Comments:

Ideas and Content: The thesis is understandable, despite misuse of the word "displays." Very little support is provided for the thesis.

Organization: The literary response includes a basic introduction and conclusion, but sentences are strung together with little attention to logical flow. Paragraphs sometimes lack a single main idea.

Voice: There is no discernible point of view, and the writing is too short to develop the topic.

Word Choice: The language is vague and imprecise. Words are used incorrectly, and pronouns are unclear.

Sentence Fluency: Sentences are monotonous and do not flow logically. Poor sentence construction and a lack of transitions impede understanding.

Conventions: Serious errors in usage, spelling, and punctuation are distracting and significantly impede understanding.

Presentation: The presentation is clear.

Persuasion: Holistic Scale

Score 4

This persuasive writing presents a clear position and supports the position with precise, relevant evidence. The reader's concerns, biases, and expectations are addressed convincingly.

- **The writing strongly demonstrates**
  - ✓ a clear understanding of all parts of the writing task
  - ✓ a meaningful thesis, a consistent tone and focus, and a purposeful control of organization
  - ✓ use of specific details and examples to support the thesis and main ideas
  - ✓ a variety of sentence types using precise, descriptive language
  - ✓ a clear understanding of audience
  - ✓ use of precise, relevant evidence to defend a position with authority, convincingly addressing the reader's concerns, biases, and expectations
  - ✓ a solid command of English-language conventions. Errors, if any, are generally minor and unobtrusive.

Score 3

This persuasive writing presents a position and supports it with evidence. The reader's concerns are addressed.

- **The writing generally demonstrates**
  - ✓ an understanding of all parts of the writing task
  - ✓ a thesis, a consistent tone and focus, and a control of organization
  - ✓ use of details and examples to support the thesis and main ideas
  - ✓ a variety of sentence types using some descriptive language
  - ✓ an understanding of audience
  - ✓ use of relevant evidence to defend a position, addressing the reader's concerns, biases, and expectations
  - ✓ an understanding of English-language conventions. Some errors exist, but they do not interfere with the reader's understanding of the essay.

Score 2

This persuasive writing presents a position, but the position is not sufficiently supported.

- **The writing demonstrates**
  - ✓ an understanding of only parts of the writing task
  - ✓ a thesis (though not always); an inconsistent tone and focus; and little, if any, control of organization
  - ✓ use of limited, if any, details and examples to support the thesis and main ideas
  - ✓ little variety in sentence types; use of basic, predictable language
  - ✓ little or no understanding of audience

132 Holt Assessment: Writing, Listening, and Speaking

Persuasion: Holistic Scale *(continued)*

	✓ use of little, if any, evidence to defend a position. The reader's concerns, biases, and expectations are not effectively addressed
	✓ inconsistent use of English-language conventions. Several errors exist and may interfere with the reader's understanding of the essay.
Score 1 **This persuasive writing may present a position, but it is not supported.**	■ *The writing lacks* ✓ an understanding of the writing task, addressing only one part ✓ a thesis (or provides only a weak thesis), a focus, and control of organization ✓ details and examples to support ideas ✓ sentence variety and uses limited vocabulary ✓ an understanding of audience ✓ evidence to defend a position and fails to address the reader's concerns, biases, and expectations ✓ an understanding of English-language conventions. Serious errors interfere with the reader's understanding of the essay.

Persuasion: Sample A

STUDENT MODEL

> **PROMPT**
>
> More and more students attend your school. You decide to write an essay for the newspaper because you think something should be done to improve the situation. Write a persuasive essay with a clear, well-supported thesis, and remember to address any possible reader concerns. Show your essay to friends who share your opinion.

How would you like your child to have to sit in a folding chair next to a bookcase just because there weren't enough student desks? If our city doesn't prepare for the growth that will result from new subdivisions, situations like this will become commonplace. Consider a scenario in which ten new housing subdivisions are built and each one has 50 houses. If half of the families who move into the houses each have two school-aged children, that's an additional 500 students who will be going to our schools. Most classrooms in our school are currently full. Even a slight increase in enrollment would cause overcrowded classrooms. We need new schools to handle increased enrollment and prevent overcrowding.

Several problems arise when there are too many students in a single classroom. Teachers have more paperwork. Because of the increased numbers of students, teachers must spend a great deal of time preparing materials, grading papers, and keeping more records. If a teacher gets three new students in one class, the teacher must spend an additional half hour grading the class's papers if he or she spends only ten minutes per paper. If that amount is multiplied by four or five classes, the teacher's workload has increased dramatically.

In addition, students need individual attention. Mr. Blakely, a sixth-grade science teacher, says, "It is especially difficult to give individual attention where it is needed. Most of a teacher's time is taken up by making sure the kids get just the basic instruction." Students who need more attention but do not receive it are in jeopardy of falling behind.

134 Holt Assessment: Writing, Listening, and Speaking

Persuasion: Sample A *(continued)*

 Traffic and safety concerns are another important reason to avoid overcrowded schools. Students are more vulnerable to traffic accidents if streets near the school are packed with increased traffic. Halls and locker areas in which students have to jostle their way to class also are potentially dangerous environments. Almost every week someone trips on the crowded stairs and twists an ankle or actually falls.

 Some people might say that building schools before there are enough students to fill the classrooms is illogical, and they would have a good point. However, we know enrollment will increase as families move into the new developments—it's just a matter of time. The importance of planning for schools in our own town is critical. If subdivisions are built before new schools are built, the problems arising from overcrowding will escalate. We do not want students to be crowded because our community leaders did not plan ahead.

 We must address school construction needs before more students are added to already crowded schools. Please express your concerns. Write letters to your city representative and attend the next school-board meeting to make sure they know we must address school construction needs now.

FOR THE TEACHER

SCORING

Persuasion: Sample A Evaluation

Holistic Scale

Rating: 4 points

Note: This essay illustrates the type of development appropriate for the prompt, but some teachers may ask their students to write longer essays.

Comments: The essay is well organized. The meaningful thesis is well supported by references to full classrooms and population growth. Sentence types are varied and use precise, descriptive language. The possible reader's concern of illogically building schools when too few students exist to fill them is convincingly addressed. The writing shows an excellent command of English-language conventions.

Analytical Scale: 7 Writing Traits

Ratings (High score is 5.)
Ideas and Content: 4
Organization: 5
Voice: 5
Word Choice: 4
Sentence Fluency: 5
Conventions: 5
Presentation: 4

Comments:

Ideas and Content: A focused thesis, the need to plan for new schools, is supported by relevant evidence. The reader's concerns are anticipated and addressed.

Organization: The essay is well organized, with an interesting introduction leading to a logical sequence of ideas.

Voice: The appropriately serious tone reveals the writer's connection to the topic.

Word Choice: Word choice is specific and effective.

Sentence Fluency: The writer uses a variety of clear, well-constructed sentences.

Conventions: The writer demonstrates a strong command of English-language conventions.

Presentation: The presentation is simple and clear.

Persuasion: Sample B

STUDENT MODEL

> **PROMPT**
>
> More and more students attend your school. You decide to write an essay for the newspaper because you think something should be done to improve the situation. Write a persuasive essay with a clear, well-supported thesis, and remember to address any possible reader concerns.

How would you like your child to be in a crowded classroom? If our city doesn't prepare for the growth that will result from new subdivisions, situations like this will become commonplace. We need more schools to prevent overcrowding.

Several problems arise when there are too many students in a single classroom. More stress, more paperwork, and additional disciplinary problems are experienced by teachers. In addition, students need individual attention. Mr. Blakely, a sixth-grade science teacher, says "it is especially difficult to give individual attention where it is needed. Most of a teacher's time is taken up by making sure the kids get just the basic instruction."

The importance of planning in our own town is critical. If the subdivisions are built before new schools are built, the problems arising from overcrowding will escelate. We do not want students to be crowded because our community leaders did not plan ahead. Some people might say that building schools before there are enough students to fill the classrooms is illogical, and they would have a good point. But we know enrollment will increase as families move into the new developments—its just a matter of time.

Every parent, teacher, and student should be concerned about the education of students in our school district. Please express your concerns.

FOR THE TEACHER

Persuasion: Sample B Evaluation

SCORING

Holistic Scale

Rating: 3 points

Comments: The thesis is clear and is supported by reasons. Sentence types are varied. The possible reader's concern of illogically building schools when too few students exist to fill them is addressed. The writing shows an understanding of English-language conventions, though some errors should have been corrected in proofreading.

Analytical Scale: 7 Writing Traits

Ratings (High score is 5.)

Ideas and Content: 3	**Sentence Fluency:** 4
Organization: 3	**Conventions:** 4
Voice: 3	**Presentation:** 4
Word Choice: 3	

Comments:

Ideas and Content: A general thesis is supported by reasons, though support could be better developed.

Organization: Basic organization is clear but could be improved by an engaging introduction, clearer transitions, and a more specific call to action.

Voice: The tone is appropriately serious, but the somewhat neutral tone rarely captivates the reader. Generalities would benefit from more detailed support.

Word Choice: Word choice is appropriate and free of jargon.

Sentence Fluency: Sentences are varied in length and construction, but better transitions would improve clarity.

Conventions: The essay contains errors in punctuation, capitalization, and spelling that should have been corrected in proofreading.

Presentation: The presentation is clear.

Persuasion: Sample C

STUDENT MODEL

> **PROMPT**
>
> More and more students attend your school. You decide to write an essay for the newspaper because you think something should be done to improve the situation. Write a persuasive essay with a clear, well-supported thesis, and remember to address any possible reader concerns.

If more people move into our town, the schools will be to full. Teacher's jobs will be harder, and students need attention. Most of a teechers time is took up by making sure the kids get just the basic instruction

If more houses are built the problems will get worse. We do not want students to be crowded because our comunity leaders didnt plan ahead. Some people might say that building schools before their is enough students is bad. They would be right? Every parent teacher and student should worrie about students in our school. Please show you're concerns.

FOR THE TEACHER

SCORING

Persuasion: Sample C Evaluation

Holistic Scale

Rating: 2 points
Comments: The thesis is vague and unsupported. The writing is poorly organized, and there is little variety in sentence structure. The possible reader's concern is conceded rather than addressed. Serious errors exist in grammar and spelling.

Analytical Scale: 7 Writing Traits

Ratings (High score is 5.)
Ideas and Content: 1   **Sentence Fluency: 2**
Organization: 2   **Conventions: 2**
Voice: 2   **Presentation: 4**
Word Choice: 2

Comments:
Ideas and Content: The thesis is vague and unsupported.
Organization: Lack of an introduction and conclusion obscures the thesis. Transitions are nonexistent.
Voice: The tone is flat, the writer's point of view is unclear, and the writing is too short to develop the topic.
Word Choice: The language is vague and uninspired.
Sentence Fluency: Sentences are monotonous and do not flow logically.
Conventions: Serious errors in grammar, spelling, and punctuation are distracting and impede understanding.
Presentation: The presentation is clear.

Business Letter: Holistic Scale

Score 4

This business letter provides clear, purposeful information. Conventional business-letter style contributes to readability and overall effect. The tone is consistent and appropriate for the intended audience.

- *The writing strongly demonstrates*
  - ✓ a clear understanding of all parts of the writing task
  - ✓ a meaningful message, a consistent tone and focus, and a purposeful control of organization
  - ✓ use of specific details and examples to support the main purpose
  - ✓ a variety of sentence types using precise, descriptive language
  - ✓ a clear understanding of audience
  - ✓ a thorough understanding of conventional business-letter style, with formats, fonts, and spacing that aid readability and have a positive overall effect
  - ✓ a solid command of English-language conventions. Errors, if any, are minor and unobtrusive.

Score 3

This business letter provides clear information. Conventional business-letter style generally contributes to readability. The tone is appropriate for the intended audience.

- *The writing generally demonstrates*
  - ✓ an understanding of all parts of the writing task
  - ✓ a clear message, a consistent tone and focus, and a control of organization
  - ✓ use of details and examples to support the purpose
  - ✓ a variety of sentence types using some descriptive language
  - ✓ an understanding of audience
  - ✓ an understanding of conventional business-letter style, with formats, fonts, and spacing that aid readability and have a positive overall effect
  - ✓ an understanding of English-language conventions. Some errors exist, but they do not interfere with the reader's understanding of the essay.

Score 2

This business letter provides somewhat vague information and strays from its focus. Conventional business-letter style is not used consistently, leaving a negative overall impression.

- *The writing demonstrates*
  - ✓ an understanding of only parts of the writing task
  - ✓ a weak message; an inconsistent tone and focus; and little, if any, control of organization
  - ✓ use of limited, if any, details and examples to support the purpose
  - ✓ little variety in sentence types and use of basic, predictable language
  - ✓ little or no understanding of audience
  - ✓ little understanding of conventional business-letter style. Formats, fonts, and spacing sometimes impede readability.
  - ✓ inconsistent use of English-language conventions. Several errors exist and may interfere with the reader's understanding of the essay.

SCALES AND SAMPLE PAPERS

Business Letter: Holistic Scale *(continued)*

Score 1

This business letter shows no understanding of business-letter purpose or style. The tone is inappropriate for the audience. Incorrect style and serious grammatical errors greatly impede readability and have an overall negative effect.

- *The writing lacks*
  - ✓ an understanding of the writing task, addressing only one part
  - ✓ a clear message, a focus, and control of organization
  - ✓ details and examples to support ideas
  - ✓ sentence variety and uses limited vocabulary
  - ✓ an understanding of audience
  - ✓ an understanding of conventional business-letter style. Formats, fonts, and spacing impede readability and have a negative overall effect.
  - ✓ an understanding of English-language conventions. Serious errors interfere with the reader's understanding of the essay.

Business Letter: Sample A

STUDENT MODEL

PROMPT

In history class one day, you learn that one of your favorite vacation spots is historically important. Write a letter of inquiry to the government office responsible for managing the area, and request more information on the historical importance of the area. Remember to use an appropriate tone and a conventional business-letter format.

2371 Lone Pine Drive
Casper, WY 82601
February 3, 2003

Oregon National Historic Trail
National Park Service
Long Distance Trails Office
324 South State Street
Suite 250
P.O. Box 45155
Salt Lake City, UT 84145-0155

Dear Sir or Madam:

I am writing in hope that you can provide me with information about the Wyoming segment of the Oregon Trail. Specifically, I would like to know where the Oregon Trail enters and exits Wyoming and the trail's path across the state. If you could send me a map of the trail or tell me where to get one, that would be even better. Is there any public access to parts of the trail in Wyoming? Is the trail marked in any way? I am especially interested in knowing if any parts of the trail still show wagon-wheel ruts worn into the ground. Also, where did the trail cross the Continental Divide?

Business Letter: Sample A *(continued)*

My history class has recently begun a study of nineteenth-century westward expansion in the United States. Having grown up in Casper, I have become fascinated with the role Wyoming—though it wasn't a state at the time—played in emigration from the eastern United States to the West. Our history teacher told us the settlers took wagons and cattle right through the Wind River Range in northwestern Wyoming. However, I have hiked in that area and wonder how wagons and cattle could make it through those mountains.

Any information you can send or references you can recommend will be greatly appreciated. My class will be studying westward expansion for three weeks. If possible, I would like the information by the end of February. Thank you for your attention to my inquiry.

Sincerely,

Brad Meeker

FOR THE TEACHER

SCORING

Business Letter: Sample A Evaluation

Holistic Scale

Rating: 4 points

Comments: This is a well-written and well-organized business letter. The block-style format is used correctly and consistently, aiding readability and leaving a favorable impression. The tone is appropriately formal for the audience of a government office. Vocabulary is simple and precise, and the letter stays focused on its purpose, requesting information about a specific segment of the Oregon Trail. Sentences are varied and clear, and English-language conventions are strictly observed.

Analytical Scale: 7 Writing Traits

Ratings (High score is 5.)

Ideas and Content: 4	**Sentence Fluency:** 5
Organization: 5	**Conventions:** 5
Voice: 5	**Presentation:** 4
Word Choice: 4	

Comments:

Ideas and Content: The letter of inquiry is well focused and clear. The writer relates personal knowledge of and interest in the subject.

Organization: The block-style format is used correctly and is appropriate for the audience. Ideas flow logically, and all elements of a business letter are present and are used appropriately.

Voice: The tone is consistently formal and respectful. The text reveals a personal dimension without becoming inappropriately informal.

Word Choice: The language is natural while remaining formal throughout. The writer uses simple, direct, and precise wording.

Sentence Fluency: The writing is clear and concise. Sentence beginnings are varied and interesting, and thoughtful transitions facilitate the logical flow of ideas.

Conventions: The writer demonstrates a strong command of English-language conventions.

Presentation: The presentation is simple and clear.

STUDENT MODEL

Business Letter: Sample B

> **PROMPT**
>
> In history class one day, you learn that one of your favorite vacation spots is historically important. Write a letter of inquiry to the government office responsible for managing the area, and request more information on the historical importance of the area. Remember to use an appropriate tone and a conventional business-letter format.

2371 Lone Pine Drive
Casper, WY 82601
February 3, 2003

Long Distance Trails Office
324 South State Street
Suite 250
P.O. Box 45155
Salt Lake City, Utah 84145

Dear sir or madam:

I am writing in hope that you can give me some information about the Wyoming part of the Oregon trail. I would like to know where the Oregon Trail enters and exits Wyoming and the trail's path across the state. If you could send me a map of the trail or tell me where to get one, that would be great.

My history class is studying nineteenth-century westward expansion in the United States. I am very interested in the role Wyoming—though it wasn't a state at the time—played in the country's growth. Our history teacher, Mr. Smithers, told us the settlers took wagons and cattle right through the Wind River Range in Northwestern Wyoming. I think Mr. Smithers is wrong because I have hiked in that area. I can't believe wagons and cattle could make it through mountains like that.

Business Letter: Sample B *(continued)*

Any information you can send or references you can recommend would be super. Someday I would like to follow the path of the entire Oregon trail, but for now I'll start with my own neck of the woods. Thanks a lot for answering my letter.

Sincerely,

Brad Meeker

FOR THE TEACHER

SCORING

Business Letter: Sample B Evaluation

Holistic Scale

Rating: 3 points

Comments: This business letter is clearly written. With the exception of the heading, which is aligned in modified block style, block-style format is used correctly and consistently. The inside address, while probably adequate, is incomplete, and the state name is spelled rather than abbreviated. The tone is generally appropriate for the audience of a government office, though the inclusion of the teacher's name, words such as *great* and *super*, the phrase "my own neck of the woods," and the closing are too informal. Vocabulary is simple and clear. English-language conventions are generally observed, with the exception of a few capitalization errors.

Analytical Scale: 7 Writing Traits

Ratings (High score is 5.)
Ideas and Content: 4   **Sentence Fluency:** 4
Organization: 3   **Conventions:** 4
Voice: 3   **Presentation:** 4
Word Choice: 3

Comments:

Ideas and Content: The letter of inquiry is clear but includes some unnecessary information. The writer relates personal knowledge of the subject.

Organization: With the exception of the heading, block-style format is used correctly. All elements of a business letter are present and are used appropriately.

Voice: The tone is mostly appropriate for the audience. The text reveals a personal dimension but occasionally is too informal.

Word Choice: The language is natural though sometimes too informal. The writer uses simple, direct wording.

Sentence Fluency: The writing is clear and concise. Sentence beginnings are varied and interesting.

Conventions: The writer demonstrates a good command of English-language conventions.

Presentation: The presentation is simple and clear.

Holt Assessment: Writing, Listening, and Speaking

STUDENT MODEL

Business Letter: Sample C

> **PROMPT**
>
> In history class one day, you learn that one of your favorite vacation spots is historically important. Write a letter of inquiry to the government office responsible for managing the area, and request more information on the historical importance of the area. Remember to use an appropriate tone and a conventional business-letter format.

2371 Lone Pine Drive
Casper, Wy 82601
Febuary 3, 2003

324 South State Street
Suite 250
P.O. Box 45155
Salt Lake City 84145

Dear sir or maddam,

I want to know about the Wyoming trail that settlers took wagons on there way to Oregon. My class studied that trail and I want to know more about Wyoming because that's where I'm from.

Tell me where the trails comes into Wyoming and where it leeves it. Do you have any map, because I want one. My teacher, Mr. Smithers, says they went right through the Wind River Mountains (I think that's in the Rockies up north). I aim to prove he's wrong because I have been there. There's now way wagons and cows could make it through mountains like them. Mr Smithers makes us take essay tests that are a lot harder than ones where you pick the answer.

If you could give me this stuff to show my class I'd be one happy camper.

Thanks a bunch!
Your pal, Brad Meeker

FOR THE TEACHER

SCORING

Business Letter: Sample C Evaluation

Holistic Scale

Rating: 2 points
Comments: This business letter is poorly written and vague. The format is inconsistent and confusing, leaving a negative impression. The heading and inside address are incomplete and contain errors. The tone is inappropriately informal. The letter contains grammatical errors that impede understanding.

Analytical Scale: 7 Writing Traits

Ratings (High score is 5.)
Ideas and Content: 2   Sentence Fluency: 1
Organization: 2   Conventions: 2
Voice: 2   Presentation: 2
Word Choice: 2

Comments:
Ideas and Content: The letter of inquiry is vague and includes unnecessary information. It is not clear what information the writer is seeking.

Organization: The format is a confusing combination of block style and modified block style. Paragraphs are inappropriately indented, and spacing between letter elements is incorrect. The closing is inappropriate and incorrectly formatted.

Voice: The tone is inappropriate for the audience. The letter contains colloquialisms such as "I aim to prove," "I'd be one happy camper," and "Thanks a bunch."

Word Choice: The language is too informal.

Sentence Fluency: The letter contains rambling sentences that do not flow logically. Little variety exists in sentence structure.

Conventions: The writer demonstrates a poor command of English-language conventions. Serious errors exist in grammar, punctuation, and capitalization.

Presentation: Inconsistencies in format leave an overall negative impression.

Portfolio Assessment

FOR THE TEACHER
Portfolio Assessment in the Language Arts

Although establishing and using a portfolio assessment system requires a certain amount of time, effort, and understanding, an increasing number of teachers believe that the benefits of implementing such a system richly reward their efforts.

Language arts portfolios are collections of materials that display aspects of students' use of language. They are a means by which students can collect samples of their written work over time so that they and their teachers can ascertain how the students are developing as language users. Because reflection and self-assessment are built-in aspects of language arts portfolios, both also help students develop their critical-thinking and metacognitive abilities.

Each portfolio collection is typically kept in a folder, box, or other container to which items are added on a regular basis. The collection can include a great variety of materials, depending on the design of the portfolio assessment program, the kinds of projects completed inside and outside the classroom, and the interests of individual students. For example, portfolios may contain student stories, essays, sketches, poems, letters, journals, and other original writing, and they may also contain reactions to articles, stories, and other texts the student has read. Other materials that are suitable for inclusion in portfolios are drawings, photographs, audiotapes, and videotapes of students taking part in special activities; clippings and pictures from newspapers and magazines; and notes on favorite authors and on stories and books that the student hopes to read. Many portfolios also include several versions of the same piece of writing, demonstrating how the writing has developed through revision.

Finally, portfolios may contain logs of things the student has read or written, written reflections or assessments of portfolio work, and tables and explanations about the way the portfolio is organized. (A collection of forms that can be used to generate these items may be found at the end of this book.)

The Advantages of Portfolio Assessment

How can portfolio assessment help you meet your instructional goals? Here are some of the most important advantages of using portfolios:

- *Portfolios link instruction and assessment.* Traditional testing is usually one or more steps removed from the process or performance being assessed. However, because portfolio assessment focuses on performance—on students' actual use of language—portfolios are a highly accurate gauge of what students have learned in the classroom.
- *Portfolios involve students in assessing their own language use and abilities.* Portfolio assessment can provide some of the most effective learning opportunities available in your classroom. In fact, the assessment is

Portfolio Assessment

FOR THE TEACHER

Portfolio Assessment in the Language Arts *(continued)*

itself instructional: Students, as self-assessors, identify their own strengths and weaknesses. Furthermore, portfolios are a natural way to develop metacognition in your students. As the collected work is analyzed, the student begins to think critically about how he or she makes meaning while reading, writing, speaking, and listening. For example, the student begins to ask questions while reading, such as "Is this telling me what I need to know?" "Am I enjoying this author as much as I expected to?" "Why or why not?" While writing, the student may ask, "Am I thinking about the goals I set when I was analyzing my portfolio?" That's what good instruction is all about: getting students to use the skills you help them develop.

- *Portfolios invite attention to important aspects of language.* Because most portfolios include numerous writing samples, they naturally direct attention to diction, style, main idea or theme, author's purpose, and other aspects of language that are difficult to assess in other ways. The portfolio encourages awareness and appreciation of these aspects of language as they occur in literature and nonfiction as well as in the student's own work.

- *Portfolios emphasize language use as a process that integrates language behaviors.* Students who keep and analyze portfolios develop an understanding that reading, writing, speaking, and listening are all aspects of a larger process. They come to see that language behaviors are connected by thinking about and expressing one's own ideas and feelings.

- *Portfolios make students aware of audience and the need for a writing purpose.* Students develop audience awareness by regularly analyzing their portfolio writing samples. Evaluation forms prompt them to reflect on whether they have defined and appropriately addressed their audience. Moreover, because portfolios provide or support opportunities for students to work together, peers can often provide feedback about how well a student has addressed an audience in his or her work. Finally, students may be asked to consider particular audiences (parents, classmates, or community groups, for example) who will review their portfolios; they may prepare explanations of the contents for such audiences, and they may select specific papers to present as a special collection to such audiences.

- *Portfolios provide a vehicle for student interaction and cooperative learning.* Many projects that normally involve group learning produce material for portfolios. Portfolios, in turn, provide or support many opportunities for students to work together. Students can work as

> As they become attuned to audience, students automatically begin to be more focused on whether their work has fulfilled their purpose for writing. They begin to ask questions like, "Did I say what I meant to say? Could I have been clearer and more effective? Do I understand what this writer wants to tell me? Do I agree with it?" Speaking and listening activities can also be evaluated in terms of audience awareness and clarity of purpose.

FOR THE TEACHER
Portfolio Assessment in the Language Arts (continued)

partners or as team members who critique each other's collections. For example, students might work together to prepare, show, and explain portfolios to particular audiences, such as parents, administrators, and other groups interested in educational progress and accountability.

- *Portfolios can incorporate many types of student expression on a variety of topics.* Students should be encouraged to include materials from different subject areas and from outside school, especially materials related to hobbies and other special interests. In this way, students come to see language arts skills as crucial tools for authentic, real-world work.
- *Portfolios provide genuine opportunities to learn about students and their progress as language users.* Portfolio contents can reveal to the teacher a great deal about the student's background and interests with respect to reading, writing, speaking, and listening. Portfolios can also demonstrate the student's development as a language user and reveal areas where he or she needs improvement.

FOR THE TEACHER

How to Develop and Use Portfolios

As you begin designing a portfolio program for your students, you may wish to read articles and reports that discuss the advantages of portfolio assessment.

Basic Design Features

For a portfolio program to be successful in the classroom, the program should reflect the teacher's particular instructional goals and the students' needs as learners. Teachers are encouraged to customize a portfolio program for their classrooms, although most successful portfolio programs share a core of essential portfolio management techniques. Following are suggestions that teachers will want to consider in customizing a portfolio program.

- *Integrate portfolio assessment into the regular classroom routine.* Teachers should make portfolio work a regular class activity by providing opportunities for students to work with their collections during class time. During these portfolio sessions, the teacher should promote analysis (assessment) that reflects his or her instructional objectives and goals.
- *Link the program to classroom activities.* Student portfolios should contain numerous examples of classroom activities and projects. To ensure that portfolios reflect the scope of students' work, some teachers require that certain papers and assignments be included.

You may want to require that certain papers, projects, and reports be included in the portfolio. Such requirements should be kept to a minimum so that students feel that they can include whatever they consider to be relevant to their language development.

- *Let students have the control.* Students can develop both self-assessment and metacognition skills when they select and arrange portfolio contents themselves. This practice also develops a strong sense of ownership: Students feel that their portfolios belong to them, not to the teacher. When students take ownership of their work, they accept more responsibility for their own language development. To encourage a sense of ownership on the part of students, portfolios should be stored where students can get at them easily, and students should have regular and frequent access to their portfolios.
- *Include students' creative efforts.* To ensure that the portfolios develop a range of language skills, encourage students to include samples of their creative writing, pieces they have written outside class, and publishing activities that they may have participated in, such as the production of a class magazine.

Portfolios that include such planning papers and intermediate drafts are called *working portfolios*. Working portfolios force the student to organize and analyze the material collected, an activity that makes clear to the student that language use is a process.

- *Make sure portfolios record students' writing process.* If portfolios are to teach language use as a process that integrates various language behaviors, they need to contain papers that show how writing grows out of planning and develops through revision. Portfolios should include notes, outlines, clippings, reactions to reading or oral presentations, pictures, and other materials that inspired the final product. Equally vital to the

FOR THE TEACHER
How to Develop and Use Portfolios (continued)

The act of selecting particular papers to show to special audiences—parents, another teacher, or the principal, to name a few—refines students' sense of audience. Preparing and presenting selected collections, called *show portfolios*, engages students in a more sophisticated analysis of their work and encourages them to visualize the audience for the show collection.

If students feel free to include writing and reading done outside class in their portfolios, you can discover interests, opinions, and concerns that can be touched on during conferences. In turn, by communicating interest in and respect for what engages the student, you can promote the success of the portfolio program.

portfolio collections are the different drafts of papers that demonstrate revision over a period of time. Such collections can promote fruitful, concrete discussions between student and teacher about how the student's process shaped the final product.

- *Rely on reactions to reading and listening.* If portfolios are to link and interrelate language behaviors, students must be encouraged to include reactions to things they read and hear. During conferences, teachers may want to point out how some of the student's work has grown out of listening or reading.
- *Encourage students to consider the audience.* Portfolio building prompts students to think about the audience because, as a kind of publication, the portfolio invites a variety of readers. Students will become interested in and sensitive to the reactions of their classmates and their teacher, as well as to the impact of the collections on any other audiences that may be allowed to view them.
- *Promote collaborative products.* Portfolios can promote student collaboration if the program sets aside class time for students to react to one another's work and to work in groups. This interaction can occur informally or in more structured student partnerships or team responses. In addition, many writing projects can be done by teams and small groups, and any common product can be reproduced for all participants' portfolios. Performance projects, speeches, and other oral presentations often require cooperative participation. Audiotapes and videotapes of group projects may be included in portfolios.
- *Let the portfolios reflect a variety of subject areas and interests.* The language arts portfolio should include material from subject areas other than language arts. Broadening the portfolio beyond the language arts classroom is important if the student is to understand that reading, writing, speaking, and listening are authentic activities—that is, that they are central to all real-world activities. Any extensive attempt to limit portfolio contents may suggest to students that these activities are important only in the language arts classroom.

Initial Design Considerations

Using what you have read so far, you can make some initial notes as guidelines for drafting your portfolio assessment design. You can complete a chart like the one on the next page to plan how you will use portfolios and what you can do to make them effective.

Portfolio Assessment

FOR THE TEACHER

How to Develop and Use Portfolios *(continued)*

▶ What are my primary goals in developing my students' ability to use language?	▶ How can portfolios contribute to meeting these goals?	▶ What design features can ensure this?

PORTFOLIO ASSESSMENT

FOR THE TEACHER

How to Develop and Use Portfolios *(continued)*

Some key considerations for designing a portfolio program have been suggested. Other considerations will arise as you assess ways to use the portfolios. Here are some questions that will probably arise in the planning stages of portfolio assessment.

How can I introduce students to the concepts of portfolio management?

What examples of student work should go into the portfolios?

What should the criteria be for deciding what will be included?

How and where will the portfolio collections be kept?

Designing a Portfolio Program

How can I introduce students to the concepts of portfolio management?

One way to introduce students to portfolios is to experiment with a group of your students. If you use this limited approach, be sure to select students with varied writing abilities to get a sense of how portfolios work for students with a range of skill levels. To introduce portfolio assessment to them, you can talk to students either individually or as a group about what they will be doing. If other students begin expressing an interest in keeping portfolios, let them take part as well. The kind of excitement that builds around portfolio keeping almost guarantees that some students not included initially will want to get on board for the trial run; some may start keeping portfolios on their own.

You might let students help you design or at least plan some details of the system. After explaining both the reasons for keeping portfolios and the elements of the program that you have decided are essential, you can let students discuss how they think certain aspects should be handled. Even if you decide you want students to make important decisions concerning the program's design, you will need to have a clear idea of what your teaching objectives are and of what you will ask students to do.

What examples of student work should go into the portfolios?

Portfolios should reflect as much as possible the spectrum of your students' language use. What you want to ensure is that student self-assessment leads to the understanding that language skills are essential to all learning. For this to happen, portfolios should contain writing, speaking, and listening activities that relate to a number of subject areas and interests, not just to the language arts. Moreover, the portfolio should include final, completed works as well as drafts, notes, freewriting, and other samples that show the student's thinking and writing process.

FINAL PRODUCTS Students should consider including pieces that are created with a general audience in mind; writing that is communicative and intended for particular audiences; and writing that is very personal and that is used as a method of thinking through situations, evaluating experiences, or musing simply for enjoyment. The portfolios can contain a variety of finished products, including

- original stories, dialogue, and scripts
- poems

Portfolio Assessment

FOR THE TEACHER

How to Develop and Use Portfolios (continued)

- essays, themes, sketches
- song lyrics
- original videos
- video or audio recordings of performances
- narrative accounts of experiences
- correspondence with family members and friends
- stream-of-consciousness pieces
- journals of various types

Examples of various types of journals that students might enjoy keeping are described below.

Keeping Journals

A journal is an excellent addition to a portfolio—and one that teachers report is very successful. Journal keeping develops the habit of recording one's observations, feelings, and ideas. At the same time, journal writing is an excellent way to develop fluency. Specifically, it can help tentative writers to overcome the reluctance to put thoughts down as words. Journal keeping can be a bridge over inhibitions to writing and can become a student's favorite example of his or her language use. These benefits support the addition of journals to the portfolio.

Success with journals in encouraging young writers has led teachers to experiment with a variety of types:

PERSONAL JOURNAL This form of journal allows the writer to make frequent entries (regularly or somewhat irregularly) on any topic and for any purpose. This popular and satisfying kind of journal writing develops writing fluency and reveals to students the essential relationship between thinking and writing. (If the journal is kept in the portfolio, you may wish to remind students that you will be viewing it. Tell students to omit anything they would not be comfortable sharing.)

LITERARY JOURNAL OR READER'S LOG This journal provides a way of promoting open-ended and freewheeling responses to student reading. Students are usually allowed to structure and organize these journals in any way that satisfies them. As a collection of written responses, the literary journal is a valuable source of notes for oral and written expression; it can also give students ideas for further reading. Finally, the literary journal is another tool that reveals to students that reading, writing, and thinking are interrelated.

TOPICAL JOURNAL This style of journal is dedicated to a particular interest or topic. It is a valuable experience for students to be allowed to express themselves freely about a specific topic—a favorite hobby, pastime, or issue, for example.

160   Holt Assessment: Writing, Listening, and Speaking

FOR THE TEACHER
How to Develop and Use Portfolios (continued)

As with the literary journal, the topical journal can point students toward project ideas and further reading.

DIALOGUE JOURNAL For this journal format, students select one person—a classmate, friend, family member, or teacher, for example—with whom to have a continuing dialogue. Dialogue journals help develop audience awareness and can promote cooperative learning. If students in your class are keeping dialogue journals with each other, be prepared to help them decide in whose portfolio the journal will go. (Because making copies may be too time consuming or expensive, you could help students arrange alternate custody, or have them experiment by keeping two distinct journals.)

Fragments and Works in Progress

Portfolios should include, in addition to finished products, papers showing how your students are processing ideas as readers, writers, speakers, and listeners. Drafts that show how writing ideas are developed through revision are especially helpful as students assess their work. Items that demonstrate how your language users are working with their collections can include

- articles, news briefs, sketches, or other sources collected and used as the basis for written or oral projects. These sources may include pictures created or collected by students and used for inspiration for the subject.
- reading-response notes that have figured in the planning of a paper and have been incorporated into the final work. Some notes may be intended for future projects.
- other notes, outlines, or evidence of planning for papers written or ready to be drafted
- pieces in which the student is thinking out a problem, considering a topic of interest or behavior, or planning something for the future. These pieces may include pro and con arguments, persuasive points, and reactions to reading.
- freewriting, done either at school or at home
- early versions (drafts) of the latest revision of a piece of writing
- notes analyzing the student's latest draft, which may direct subsequent revision
- solicited reactions from classmates or the teacher
- a published piece accompanied by revised manuscripts showing edits

Portfolio Assessment

FOR THE TEACHER
How to Develop and Use Portfolios *(continued)*

- correspondence from relatives and friends to which students have written a response or to which students need to respond
- journal or diary entries that are equivalent to preliminary notes or drafts of a piece of writing
- tapes of conversations or interviews to which a piece of writing refers or on which it is based

While test results in general do not make good contents for portfolios, performance assessments can provide a focused example of both language processing and integration of reading and writing skills. Such performance tests are now frequently structured as realistic tasks that require reading, synthesizing, and reacting to particular texts. More often than not, these assessments guide the student through planning stages and a preliminary draft. (These parts of the assessment are rarely rated, but they lend themselves directly to self-analysis and should definitely be included with the final draft.)

What should the criteria be for deciding what will be included?

Teachers often want to ensure that students keep certain kinds of papers in the portfolios, while also affirming students' need for a genuine sense of ownership of their collections. Achieving a balance between these two general objectives may not be as difficult as it seems. Students can be informed at the time that they are introduced to the portfolio concept that they will be asked to keep certain items as one part of the overall project. Almost certainly, it will be necessary to explain at some point that the collections are to be working portfolios and that certain records—including many of the forms provided in this booklet—will also need to be included. As they become accustomed to analyzing the papers in their portfolios, students can be encouraged or required to select the contents of their portfolios, using criteria that they develop themselves. Teachers can help students articulate these criteria in informal and formal conferences. Following are criteria teachers or students might consider:

- papers that students think are well done and that therefore represent their best efforts, or papers that were difficult to complete
- subjects that students enjoyed writing about, or texts they have enjoyed reading; things that they think are interesting or will interest others
- things that relate to reading or writing that students intend to do in the future, including ideas that may be developed into persuasive essays, details to support positions on issues, and reactions to favorite literary texts

Discourage the inclusion of workbook sheets, unless they contain ideas for future student writing; they tend to obscure the message that language development is a process, a major component of which is the expression of student ideas and opinions.

You might want to brainstorm a list of things that could be kept in your students' portfolios and then prioritize the items on your list according to which ones you think will be essential for students' development.

FOR THE TEACHER
How to Develop and Use Portfolios (continued)

- papers that contain ideas or procedures that students wish to remember
- incomplete essays or projects that presented some problem for the student. He or she may plan to ask a parent, teacher, or fellow student to react to the work or to earlier drafts.
- work that students would like particular viewers of the portfolio (the teacher, their parents, their classmates, and so on) to see, for some reason. This criterion is one that will dictate selections for a show portfolio; it may also determine some of the papers selected for the overall collection.

After building their collections for some time, students should be able to examine them and make lists of their selection criteria in their own words. Doing so should balance out any requirements the teacher has set for inclusion and should ensure students' sense of ownership.

A final note on selection criteria for student portfolios: While portfolios should certainly contain students' best efforts, too often teachers and students elect to collect only their "best stuff." An overemphasis on possible audiences that might view the collection can make it seem important that the collection be a show portfolio. Preparing show portfolios for particular audiences can require students to assess their work in order to decide what is worth including. That is a worthwhile experience, but once the preparation for the show has been completed, student self-assessment ends.

How and where will the portfolio collections be kept?

Part of the fun of keeping portfolios is deciding what the holders for the collections will look like. In a few classrooms, portfolio holders are standardized, but in most classes, the students are allowed to create their own. Many teachers allow students to furnish their own containers or folders, as long as these are big enough to hold the collections without students' having to fold or roll the papers—and not so large as to create storage problems. In addition, many teachers encourage their students to decorate their portfolio holders in unique, colorful, personal, and whimsical ways. Allowing this individuality creates enthusiasm for the project. It also helps students develop a genuine sense of ownership, an important attitude to foster if this system is to succeed.

The kinds of holders that students are likely to bring to school include household cardboard boxes, stationery boxes, folders of various types, paper or plastic shopping bags, computer paper boxes, and plastic and cardboard containers for storing clothing and other items. It would be a good idea to

Start collecting some samples of holders you can show when you introduce portfolio management to your students. Decorate at least one sample, or have a young friend or relative do it. At the same time, be thinking about areas in your classroom where the collections can be kept.

Portfolio Assessment **163**

FOR THE TEACHER
How to Develop and Use Portfolios (continued)

have several different examples to show students when discussing how they will keep their papers. It is also a good idea to have some holders on hand for students who are unable to find anything at home that they think is suitable, and for use as replacements for unworkable holders some students may bring, such as shoe boxes that are too small to hold the portfolio items.

The resulting storage area will probably not be neatly uniform but will not necessarily be unattractive, either. Teachers who want a tidier storage area might find similar boxes to pass out to all students, who are then allowed to personalize them in different ways.

The amount of space available in a particular classroom will, of course, determine where students keep their collections, but it is vital that the area be accessible to students. It will save a great deal of inconvenience during the school year if the portfolios are on open shelves or on an accessible ledge of some kind and are not too far from students. If students can retrieve and put away their portfolios in less than a minute or two, there will be many instances when portfolio work can be allowed. Deciding where to keep the portfolios is a decision that may be put off until students know enough about the process to help make the decision.

Open access to portfolios does create the possibility of students looking at classmates' collections without permission and without warning. Remind students not to include in their portfolio anything they would not want others to see. A caution from the teacher could save a student from a wounding embarrassment.

FOR THE TEACHER
Conferencing with Students

If you are new at conducting portfolio conferences, ask a student who has kept one or more papers to sit down and talk with you. Talk with the student about what he or she thinks is strong about the paper, how it came to be written, and what kind of reading or research the student undertook. See how well you can promote an open-ended conversation related to the topic of the paper and to language use.

The regular informal exchanges between teacher and student about portfolio content are obviously very important, but the more formal conferences that anchor a successful program are of equal if not greater importance. Conferences are evidence that both the teacher and the student take the portfolio collection seriously and that the usefulness of the portfolio depends on an ongoing analysis of it. By blocking out time to conduct at least four formal conferences with each student each year, the teacher demonstrates a commitment to the program and a genuine interest in each student's progress.

Conducting Portfolio Conferences

The conference should proceed as a friendly but clearly directed conversation between the student and the teacher. The focus of the conference should be on how the use of language serves the student's needs and interests. This focus translates, in the course of the conference, into helping each student reflect on why and how he or she reads and writes.

Teachers will want to discuss with students the quantity of recent writing compared with that of previous time periods, the kinds of writing that the student has done, and the student's purposes for writing. Teachers will also want to discuss how the inclusions in the portfolio came to be and whether the pieces represent experiences and ideas the student has enjoyed and thinks are important. Teachers should let students know that the portfolio documents say something important about the individual student's life. In fact, a significant portion of the conference may be dedicated to learning about the student's interests. Here are a few examples of the types of statements that might elicit a helpful response:

- You seem to know a lot about deep-sea diving.
- Where did you learn all those details?
- Have you looked for books about deep-sea diving?
- What kinds of things could you write about deep-sea diving?

Think about what you could do to ensure a productive portfolio conference that would be helpful and worthwhile to students.

The student, too, should feel free to ask questions:

- Which pieces seem the best to the teacher and why?
- Is it always necessary to write for an audience?
- What if I *want* an idea or thought to remain private, though written?
- If I don't know how to spell a certain word, is it OK to just keep writing and look it up later?

Portfolio Assessment

FOR THE TEACHER

Conferencing with Students (continued)

These examples show how the conference can provide powerful, effective opportunities to teach and to guide language development. The conference conversations between the teacher and the student should be as unique as the individual student who joins the teacher in this exchange.

Ideally, each student will look forward to the conference as a time when student and teacher pay close attention to what the student has done; how the student feels about that performance; and what the student's needs and goals are. Such conferences encourage students to accept responsibility for their own development.

The following guidelines will help the teacher make the most of portfolio conferences.

Conference Guidelines

- *Conferences should be conducted without interruption.* Plan creatively: Perhaps a volunteer assistant can manage the rest of the class during meetings. Or, assign to other students learning activities or other work that does not disrupt your exchange with the student. It may be necessary to conduct the conference outside class time.

- *Keep the focus on the student.* Make the conference as much like an informal conversation as possible by asking questions that will emphasize the student's interests, attitudes toward writing, and favorite topics. Demonstrate that you care about what the student thinks and likes. You can also show that you respect the way a student's individuality is manifested in language use.

- *Let the conversation develop naturally.* Be an active listener: Give full attention to what the student is saying. The student's contribution is likely to suggest a question or comment from you, resulting in a genuine and natural exchange. There may be opportunities to get back to questions you had hoped to ask, but teachers should respect the course that the exchange takes and realize that some of their planned questions will need to be dropped. Good listening on the part of the teacher will help create successful conferences that address individual student interests and needs.

- *Be sincere but not judgmental.* Avoid evaluating or passing judgment on interests or aspects of the student's language use. On the other hand, try to avoid continually expressing approval and thereby creating a situation in which the student tries to respond in a way that will win favor: The conference will then lose its focus on the individual's language needs and development.

For many teachers, the time and planning that the conference demands constitute the most difficult aspect of portfolio assessment. Think about how you can use all the resources at your disposal, and don't forget to enlist students' help. Ask them to help you schedule meetings, and request their cooperation so that the system functions smoothly.

Questions will undoubtedly occur to you while reviewing the student's portfolio. It may be useful to have a few notes to remind you of things you would like to ask. Do not, however, approach a conference with a list that dictates the exchange with the student.

FOR THE TEACHER

Conferencing with Students *(continued)*

Don't hesitate to use the conference as a means of getting to know the student better by learning about his or her interests, pastimes, concerns, and opinions. This can be time well spent, particularly if it demonstrates to the student that the various aspects of his or her life can be very closely connected to the use and development of language arts skills.

Shortly after the conference, the student can translate his or her notes to a worksheet like the goal-setting form in this book, which will ask the student to elaborate on the objectives that have been established.

- *Keep the conversation open and positive.* It is fine to ask questions that direct the focus back to the collection, as long as that leads in turn to a discussion of ideas and content, the process of writing, and indications of the student's strengths and progress as a language user. In general, however, teachers should ask questions that promise to open up discussion, not shut it down. Phrase questions and comments so that they invite elaboration and explanation.
- *Gear the conference toward goal setting.* Identify and come to an agreement about the goals and objectives the student will be working on during the next time period.
- *Limit the attention devoted to usage errors.* If the student needs to focus on mechanical or grammatical problems, suggest that over the next time period the student pay particular attention to these problems when editing and revising. Do not, however, turn the session into a catalogue of language errors encountered. Keep in mind that if there are four conferences and each one tactfully encourages a focus on just one or two examples of non-standard mechanical usage, it is possible to eliminate from four to eight high-priority errors during the course of a school year.
- *Keep joint notes with the student on the conference.* To keep a focus on the most important aspects of the conference, you and the student should keep notes. Frequently, student and teacher will record notes based on the same observation: For example, the student might write, "I like to use a lot of verbs at the beginning of my sentences, but maybe I use too many." And the teacher might write, "Let's watch to see how often Cody frontshifts sentence elements for emphasis." The student might write, "Look for a novel about the Civil War." The teacher might note, "Find a copy of *The Killer Angels* for Cody if possible." When the two participants make notes on the same sheet, side by side, the notes on the same point will roughly correspond. The teacher and the student can even write at the same time if they can position the note sheet in a way that will facilitate this.

Keep in mind that conference notes frequently serve as a reference point for an action plan that is then more fully considered on the goal-setting worksheet.

Types of Student-Teacher Conferences

In addition to the scheduled conference, there are several other types of conferences that teachers can conduct as a part of portfolio assessment:

FOR THE TEACHER

Conferencing with Students *(continued)*

GOAL CLARIFICATION CONFERENCES If a student appears to be having trouble using the portfolio system, a goal clarification conference can be scheduled. The meeting's focus should be to help the student clarify and articulate objectives so that work on the collection is directed and productive.

It is important that this session not be perceived as being overly critical of the student. Be supportive and positive about the collection; try to generate a discussion that will lead to clear goals for the student. These objectives can be articulated on a goal-setting worksheet, which the teacher can help the student fill out.

PUBLICATION STAFF CONFERENCES Students who are publishing pieces they write may frequently meet as teams or in staff conferences to select pieces from their portfolios. They may also discuss possible revisions of manuscripts they hope to publish. Teachers may enjoy observing and even participating in these but should let students direct them as much as possible.

Other class projects and collaborative activities can generate similar student conferences that may involve portfolio collections.

INFORMAL OR ROVING CONFERENCES In these conferences, teachers consult with students about their portfolios during impromptu sessions. For example, at any time a teacher might encounter a student with an important and intriguing question, or spot confusion or a situation developing into frustration for a self-assessor. Often the situation calls for effective questioning and then good listening, just as in the regularly scheduled conferences.

FOR THE TEACHER
Questions and Answers

The questions that follow are frequently asked by teachers who are thinking about instituting a portfolio management system.

- How can I make my students familiar and comfortable with the idea of creating portfolios?
- How often should my students work on their portfolios?
- How can I keep the portfolios from growing too bulky to manage and analyze effectively?
- Should I grade my students' portfolios?
- Who else, besides the student and me, should be allowed to see the portfolio?
- How can I protect against the possible negative effects of allowing a wide variety of persons to see students' portfolios?

How can I make my students comfortable with portfolios?

Teachers will, of course, want to begin by describing what portfolios are and what they are designed to accomplish. One way to help students visualize portfolios is to point out that some professionals keep portfolios:

- Artists usually keep portfolios to show prospective clients or employers what kind of work they can do. In a sense, an artist's studio is one big working portfolio, full of projects in various stages of completion.
- Photographers, architects, clothing designers, interior designers, and a host of other professionals keep portfolios full of samples of their work.
- Models carry portfolios of pictures showing them in a variety of styles and situations.
- Some writers keep portfolios of their work.
- People who invest their money in stocks and bonds call a collection of different investments a portfolio.

Teachers can encourage students' interest by inviting to the classroom someone who can exhibit and explain a professional portfolio. Teachers might also show students an actual language arts portfolio created by a student in another class or school. Some teachers put together a portfolio of their own and use it as an example for their students.

After this or another introduction, you might share the following information with students:

- Explain what kinds of things will go into the portfolios and why. Students can choose what to include in their collections, but teachers can indicate that a few items will be required, including some records. Without introducing all the records to be used, teachers might show and explain basic forms, such as logs. If forms filled out by students are available, use them as examples.

Portfolio Assessment

FOR THE TEACHER

Questions and Answers (continued)

- Stress that portfolios will be examined regularly. If the working portfolios will be available to parents or others, be sure to inform students. If you plan for others to see only show portfolios, this might be a good time to introduce this kind of portfolio.

- Show examples of holders that might be used, and explain where they will be kept. Students can be involved in making decisions about how and where portfolios will be housed.

How often should my students work on their portfolios?

The answer is "regularly and often." Teachers should schedule half-hour sessions weekly; ideally, there will be time almost every day when students can work on their collections. The Scheduling Plan on the next page shows activities that should occur regularly in your program.

How can I keep the portfolios from growing too bulky to manage and analyze effectively?

Because portfolios are intended to demonstrate students' products and processes over time, collections should be culled only when necessary. However, working portfolios can become simply too big, bulky, and clumsy to organize and analyze. If some students find their collections too unwieldy to work with, encourage them to try one of the following techniques:

- Cull older pieces except for those that stand as the best work examples. Put the removed contents into a separate holder and complete an *About This Portfolio* record. Explain on the record that the work consists of less-favored work, and have students take it home for parents to examine and/or save. Photocopies of later work that you consider more successful can be included as comparison.

- Close the whole collection, except for writing not yet completed, notes and records the student intends to use, and other idea files. Send the entire collection home with an explanation record, and start a new portfolio.

- Cull from the collection one or more show portfolios for particular audiences, such as parents, other relatives, other teachers, administrators, or supervisors. After the show portfolio has been viewed, return it to the rest of the collection. Start a new portfolio, beginning with the ideas in progress.

Some teachers have their students prepare a larger decorated box to take home at the beginning of the school year. This container eventually holds banded groups of papers culled during the year. Students then have one repository for their entire portfolio collection, which they can keep indefinitely.

FOR THE TEACHER

Questions and Answers *(continued)*

SCHEDULING PLAN FOR PORTFOLIO ASSESSMENT

Activity	Frequency	The Student	The Teacher
Keeping logs	As writing and other language experiences are completed; daily if necessary	Makes the entries on the *Writing Record*	Encourages the student to make regular entries and discusses with the student indications of progress, developing interests, etc.
Collecting writing samples, reactions to reading, entries that reflect on oral language	As drafts and reactions to reading become available; can be as often as daily	Selects materials to be included	Can select materials to be included; may require some inclusions
Keeping journal(s)	Ongoing basis; daily to at least once a week	Makes regular entries in one or more journals	Analyzes journal writing discreetly and confidentially
Adding notes, pictures, clippings, and other idea sources	Weekly or more often	Clips and collects ideas and adds them to appropriate place in the portfolio	Reacts to student's idea sources (every month or so); discusses with student how he or she will use them
Explaining, analyzing, evaluating inclusions	Weekly; at least every other week	Uses forms for evaluating and organizing work to analyze and describe individual pieces included	Analyzes inclusions and student analysis of them at least four times a year—before conferences
Completing summary analyses	Monthly and always before conference	Completes a *Summary of Progress* record while comparing it with previously completed summary	Completes selected progress reports at least four times a year—before conferences, relying on student summaries and previously completed records
Conferencing—informal	Ongoing; ideally, at least once a week	Freely asks teacher for advice as often as needed; shares emerging observations with teacher	Makes an effort to observe student working on portfolio at least every two weeks and to discuss one or more specific new inclusions and analyses
Conferencing—formal	At least four times a year	Prepares for conference by completing summaries; discusses portfolio contents and analysis of them with teacher; devises new goals; takes joint notes	Prepares for conference with evaluative analyses; discusses portfolio contents and analysis with student; establishes new goals; takes joint notes
Preparing explanation of portfolio and analysis of it for a particular audience	As occasion for allowing other audiences access arises	Thoughtfully fills out the *About This Portfolio* form	Keeps student advised as to when other audiences might be looking at the student's collection and who the viewer(s) will be
Reacting to a fellow student's paper or portfolio	When it is requested by a "partner" or other classmate	Conferences with peer	Encourages collaboration whenever possible

Portfolio Assessment

FOR THE TEACHER

Questions and Answers *(continued)*

Should I grade my students' portfolios?

Teachers might be tempted to grade portfolios to let students know that they are accountable for their work; teachers may also feel that a grade legitimizes—or at least recognizes—the time and effort that goes into successful portfolio assessment. Finally, many parents, school supervisors, and administrators will expect the teacher to grade the portfolio. These reasons notwithstanding, most portfolio experts recommend that portfolios not be graded. Keep in mind that the collection will contain papers that have been graded. A grade for the collection as a whole, however, risks undermining the goals of portfolio management. Grading portfolios may encourage students to include only their "best" work, and that practice may convey the message that student self-assessment is not taken seriously. Think about it: How would you feel if someone decided to incorporate your journal entries, your collection of ideas that interest you, and other notes and informal jottings into a package that was being rated and given a grade?

Who, besides the student and me, should see the portfolio?

This question raises some of the same concerns as the issue of grading portfolios. Teachers may feel some responsibility to let parents, a supervisor, the principal, and fellow faculty members know how the program is proceeding and what it shows about the progress of individuals or of the class as a whole. It is important to balance the benefits of showing portfolios to outside audiences against the possible adverse effects—the risk of inhibiting students, diminishing their sense of ownership, or invading their privacy. Above all, the primary aims of portfolio assessment must be kept in mind.

Following are some suggestions for showing portfolios, with respect to the audience involved.

> Another way to involve parents in portfolio management is to let students plan a workshop on portfolio management geared for parents and others who are interested. Or, as suggested earlier, have students cull their collections periodically and take the materials home for their parents to see.

PARENTS OR GUARDIANS Family members will almost certainly be viewing the portfolio in one form or another. If parents or other responsible adults are to view collections only on more formal occasions, such as back-to-school night or during unscheduled visits to the classroom, then students should be assisted in creating show portfolios. If, on the other hand, the teacher will show students' portfolios without the owners' knowledge or without offering them the opportunity to review the contents beforehand, the teacher must tell students this at the beginning of the year. Warning students of these unscheduled viewings may qualify their sense of ownership; it can also intensify their audience awareness.

FOR THE TEACHER

Questions and Answers *(continued)*

Again, if portfolios will be shown to other educators, students should be made aware of this before they start to build their collections.

SCHOOL SUPERVISORS AND PRINCIPALS Students' portfolios can demonstrate to fellow educators how youngsters develop as language users, thinkers, and people; they can also show the kind of learning that is taking place in the classroom. When working portfolios are shown, they are usually selected at random from those kept in the class, and the owner's identity is masked. Show portfolios are usually prepared specifically for this purpose. Whether teachers use working or show collections (assuming the state or school system does not mandate one) may depend partly on whether they think the audience will be able to appreciate that the working collections show process.

CLASSMATES Students may review their peers' portfolios as part of the program's assessment. Even if a particular program does not include a formal peer-review stage, remind students that peers may see their collections—either in the process of collaborative work or peer review, or because a student does not respect the privacy of others.

NEXT YEAR'S TEACHERS At the end of the school year, teachers can help students create a show portfolio for their next teacher or teachers. These portfolios should demonstrate the student's growth during the year and the potential of his or her best efforts. They should also indicate the most recent goals established by the teacher and the student, so that the new teacher knows how the student sees his or her language skills developing over the next year.

Encourage students to include finished projects as well as earlier drafts. Discuss what kinds of logs should be included, or have students prepare a brief report showing how goals have been met. A fresh table of contents would be useful, as would an explanation of what the show collection includes and what its purpose is. Teachers may want to let students make copies of some papers that they would also like to take home.

THE STUDENTS THEMSELVES At the end of the school year, portfolio contents can be sent home for parents to see and save, if they wish. Before doing this, teachers may wish to have students prepare a starter portfolio of ideas, writing, plans for reading, and so on, for next year.

How can I protect against the possible negative effects of allowing a wide variety of persons to see students' portfolios?

Whatever special reporting the teacher does with portfolios, he or she needs to offset any possible adverse effects by keeping the primary aims for portfolio assessment in mind.

FOR THE TEACHER

Questions and Answers *(continued)*

- The overall goal of the program is to develop students as language users. That goal should become the focus of joint student/teacher evaluation of the student's progress.
- Because another important goal is for students to develop a habit of self-assessment, the collections must be readily available to students.
- The emphasis should be on examining the process by looking at the product and the way it is produced. Each portfolio should be a working collection containing notes, drafts, and records of the evaluation of its contents.
- The activities assessed should integrate reading, writing, speaking, and listening.
- The portfolio should be controlled and owned by the student.
- The collections should include reactions to and applications of a variety of text and writing types—with a variety of purposes involving different audiences.

NAME _____ CLASS _____

Portfolio Table of Contents

Decide on the major categories for work in your portfolio. Then, in the sections below, list the categories you have chosen. The works themselves may be papers, speech notecards, videotapes, multimedia products, or any work you and your teacher agree should be included. In choosing categories, consider organizing work by topic, by genre (essays, poems, stories, and so on), by chronology (work completed by month, for example), by level of difficulty (work that was less difficult, somewhat difficult, and more difficult), or according to another plan.

Grade: _____ School year: _____

▶ WORK IN EACH SECTION	▶ WHY I PUT THIS WORK IN THIS SECTION
Section 1:	
title:	
title:	
title:	
title:	
Section 2:	
title:	
title:	
title:	
title:	
Section 3:	
title:	
title:	
title:	
title:	

Portfolio Assessment

NAME _____ CLASS _____ DATE _____

SELF-EVALUATION

About This Portfolio

Use this form whenever you are preparing your portfolio for review by your teacher or another reader.

Grade: _____ **School year:** _____ **When I began this portfolio:** _____

▶ **How it is organized:**

▶ **What I think it shows about my progress . . .**

as a reader:

as a writer:

as a listener:

as a speaker:

GO ON ▶

PORTFOLIO ASSESSMENT

176 Holt Assessment: Writing, Listening, and Speaking

NAME _____ CLASS _____ DATE _____

SELF-EVALUATION

About This Portfolio *(continued)*

▶ **Examples of My Best Work**

The best things I have read are—	Why I like them—
The best things I have written are—	Why I like them—
Other things in my portfolio that I hope you notice are— 1. 2. 3.	What they show—

Portfolio Assessment **177**

STUDENT'S NAME _____ CLASS _____ DATE _____

TO PARENT OR GUARDIAN

Home Review: What the Portfolio Shows

In the left-hand column of the chart below, I have noted what I believe this portfolio shows about your child's development in areas such as reading, writing, speaking, and listening. The right-hand column notes where you can look for evidence of that development.

    A prime objective in keeping portfolios is to develop in students a habit of analyzing and evaluating their work. This portfolio includes work that the student has collected over a period of time. The student has decided what to include but has been encouraged to include different types of writing, responses to reading, and evidence of other uses of language. Many of the writings included are accompanied by earlier drafts and plans that show how the work has evolved from a raw idea to a finished piece of writing. The inclusion of drafts is intended to reinforce to the student that using language entails a process of revision and refinement.

▶ I believe that this portfolio shows—	▶ To see evidence of this, please notice—

Teacher's signature _____

178   Holt Assessment: Writing, Listening, and Speaking

| STUDENT'S NAME | CLASS | DATE |

TO PARENT OR GUARDIAN

Home Response to the Portfolio

▶ Please answer any questions that seem important to you. Use the reverse side for any additional comments or questions.

Parent or Guardian _____ Date _____

What did you learn from the portfolio about your child's reading?
_____
_____
_____

What did you learn from the portfolio about your child's writing?
_____
_____
_____

Were you surprised by anything in the portfolio? Why?
_____
_____

What do you think is the best thing in the portfolio? What do you like about it?
_____
_____
_____

Do you have questions about anything in the portfolio? What would you like to know more about?
_____
_____
_____

What does the portfolio tell you about your child's progress as a writer, reader, and thinker?
_____
_____
_____

Do you think keeping a portfolio has had an effect on your child as a reader or writer—or in another way? If so, what?
_____
_____
_____
_____

Is there anything missing from the portfolio that you would have liked or had expected to see? If so, what?
_____
_____

PORTFOLIO ASSESSMENT

Portfolio Assessment

NAME　　　　　　　　　　　　　　　　CLASS　　　　　　　　　　　　　SCHOOL YEAR

SELF-EVALUATION

Writing Record

Ratings: ✓✓✓✓ One of my best!　　　✓✓ OK, but not my best
　　　　　　✓✓✓ Better if I revise it　　　✓ I don't like this one.

Month/Day	Title and type of writing	Notes about this piece of writing	Rating

PORTFOLIO ASSESSMENT

180 Holt Assessment: Writing, Listening, and Speaking

NAME _____ CLASS _____ SCHOOL YEAR _____

SELF-EVALUATION

Spelling Log

▶ Word	▶ My misspelling	▶ How to remember correct spelling

PORTFOLIO ASSESSMENT

NAME _____ CLASS _____ SCHOOL YEAR _____

Goal-Setting for Writing, Listening, and Speaking

GOAL	STEPS TO REACH GOAL	REVIEW OF PROGRESS
Writing Goals		

GO ON

182 Holt Assessment: Writing, Listening, and Speaking

NAME _____ CLASS _____ SCHOOL YEAR _____

Goal-Setting for Writing, Listening, and Speaking *(continued)*

▶ GOAL	▶ STEPS TO REACH GOAL	▶ REVIEW OF PROGRESS
Listening Goals		
Speaking Goals		

Portfolio Assessment

NAME _____ CLASS _____

SELF-EVALUATION

Summary of Progress: Writing, Listening, and Speaking

Complete this form before sitting down with your teacher or a classmate to assess your overall progress, set goals, or discuss specific pieces of your work.

Grade: _____ School year: _____ Date of summary: _____

▶ **What work have I done so far this year?**

Writing:

Listening:

Speaking:

▶ **What project do I plan to work on next?**

Writing:

Listening:

Speaking:

▶ **What do I think of my progress?**

What about my work has improved?

What needs to be better?

▶ **Which examples of work are my favorites and why?**

PORTFOLIO ASSESSMENT

184 Holt Assessment: Writing, Listening, and Speaking

NAME _____ CLASS _____

SELF-EVALUATION

Summary of Progress: Writing, Listening, and Speaking *(continued)*

▶ **Which pieces of work need more revision, and what is needed?**

▶ **How has listening or speaking helped me in preparing for papers or other projects this year?**

▶ **What a classmate or the teacher thinks about my progress**

In writing—

In listening—

In speaking—

GO ON

Portfolio Assessment **185**

NAME _____ CLASS _____ DATE _____

SELF-EVALUATION

Writing Self-Inventory

▶ Questions and answers about my writing	▶ More about my answers
How often do I write?	What types of writing do I do?
Where, besides school, do I write?	What kind of writing do I do there?
Do I like to write?	Why or why not?
Of the things I have written, I like these best:	Why do I like them best?
What topics do I like to write about?	Why do I like to write about these topics?
Is anything about writing difficult for me? What?	Why do I think it is difficult?
Does reading help me to be a better writer or vice versa?	Why do I think this?
How important is learning to write well?	Why do I think this?

PORTFOLIO ASSESSMENT

186 Holt Assessment: Writing, Listening, and Speaking

NAME _____ CLASS _____ DATE _____

SELF-EVALUATION

Writing Process Self-Evaluation

Choose one paper from your portfolio, preferably one for which you have your prewriting notes and all your drafts. Use the chart below to analyze your writing process. Circle the numbers that most clearly indicate how well you meet the stated criteria in your writing process. The lowest possible total score is 5, the highest, 20.

1 = Do not meet these criteria
2 = Attempt to meet these criteria but need to improve
3 = Are fairly successful in meeting criteria
4 = Clearly meet these criteria

Title of paper _____

▶ STAGE IN WRITING PROCESS	▶ CRITERIA FOR EVALUATION	▶ RATING
Prewriting	▪ Use prewriting techniques to find and limit subject and to gather details about subject ▪ Organize details in a reasonable way	1 2 3 4
Writing	▪ Get most of ideas down on paper in a rough draft	1 2 3 4
Revising	▪ Do complete peer- or self-evaluation ▪ Find ways to improve content, organization, and style of rough draft ▪ Revise by adding, cutting, replacing, and moving material	1 2 3 4
Proofreading	▪ Correct errors in spelling, grammar, usage, punctuation, capitalization, and manuscript form	1 2 3 4
Publishing and Reflecting	▪ Produce a clean final copy in proper form ▪ Share the piece of writing with others ▪ Reflect on the writing process and on the paper's strengths and weaknesses	1 2 3 4

Additional Comments:

Portfolio Assessment

NAME _____ CLASS _____ DATE _____

SELF-EVALUATION

Proofreading Strategies

Proofread your paper using one of the following steps. Put a check by the step you used.

_____ **1.** Read the paper backward word by word.

_____ **2.** Make a large card with a one- or two-inch-sized strip cut into it and read every word in the paper, one at a time, through the hole.

_____ **3.** Read the first sentence in your paper carefully. Put your left index finger on the punctuation mark that signals the end of that sentence. Now, put your right index finger on the punctuation mark that ends the second sentence. Carefully read the material between your fingers; then, move your left index finger to the end of the second sentence and your right to the end of the third sentence, and read carefully. Keep moving your fingers until you have carefully examined each sentence in the paper.

List the mistakes you discovered when proofreading.

_____

_____

_____

_____

_____

_____

_____

_____

_____

_____

_____

_____

_____

188 Holt Assessment: Writing, Listening, and Speaking

NAME _____ CLASS _____ DATE _____

PEER- AND SELF-EVALUATION

Proofreading Checklist

Read through the paper and then mark the following statements either **T** for true or **F** for false. If you are reviewing a classmate's paper, return the paper and checklist to the writer. After the writer has done his or her best to correct the paper, offer to assist if your help is needed.

Writer's name _____ Title of paper _____

_____ 1. The paper is neat.

_____ 2. Each sentence begins with a capital letter.

_____ 3. Each sentence ends with a period, question mark, or exclamation mark.

_____ 4. Each sentence is complete. Each has a subject and a predicate and expresses a complete thought.

_____ 5. Run-on sentences are avoided.

_____ 6. A singular verb is used with each singular subject and a plural verb with each plural subject.

_____ 7. Nominative case pronouns such as *I* and *we* are used for subjects; objective case pronouns such as *me* and *us* are used for objects.

_____ 8. Singular pronouns are used to refer to singular nouns, and plural pronouns are used to refer to plural nouns.

_____ 9. Indefinite pronoun references are avoided.

_____ 10. Each word is spelled correctly.

_____ 11. Frequently confused words, such as *lie/lay*, *sit/set*, *rise/raise*, *all ready/already*, and *fewer/less*, are used correctly.

_____ 12. Double negatives are avoided.

_____ 13. All proper nouns and proper adjectives are capitalized.

_____ 14. Word endings such as *–s*, *–ing*, and *–ed* are included where they should be.

_____ 15. No words have been accidentally left out or accidentally written twice.

_____ 16. Each paragraph is indented.

_____ 17. Apostrophes are used correctly with contractions and possessive nouns.

_____ 18. Commas or pairs of commas are used correctly.

_____ 19. Dialogue is punctuated and capitalized correctly.

_____ 20. Any correction that could not be rewritten or retyped is crossed out with a single line.

NAME _____ CLASS _____ DATE _____

PEER- AND SELF-EVALUATION

Record of Proofreading Corrections

Keeping a record of the kinds of mistakes you make can be helpful. For the next few writing assignments, list the errors you, your teacher, or your peers find in your work. If you faithfully use this kind of record, you'll find it easier to avoid troublesome errors.

Writer's name _____ Title of paper _____

Write sentences that contain errors in grammar or usage here. **Write corrections here.**

Write sentences that contain errors in mechanics here. **Write corrections here.**

Write misspelled words and corrections here.

PORTFOLIO ASSESSMENT

190 Holt Assessment: Writing, Listening, and Speaking

NAME _____ CLASS _____ DATE _____

SELF-EVALUATION

Multiple-Assignment Proofreading Record

▶ **DIRECTIONS:** When your teacher returns a corrected writing assignment, write the title or topic on the appropriate vertical line at right. Under the title or topic, record the number of errors you made in each area. Use this sheet when you proofread your next assignment, taking care to check those areas in which you make frequent mistakes.

▶ **TITLE OR TOPIC OF ASSIGNMENT**

Type of Error									
Sentence Fragments									
Run-on Sentences									
Subject-Verb Agreement									
Pronoun Agreement									
Incorrect Pronoun Form									
Use of Double Negative									
Comparison of Adjectives and Adverbs									
Confusing Verbs									
Irregular Verbs									
Noun Plurals and Possessives									
Capitalization									
Spelling									
End Punctuation									
Apostrophes									
Confusing Words									
Quotation Marks and Italics									
Comma or Paired Commas									

PORTFOLIO ASSESSMENT

Portfolio Assessment **191**

NAME _____ CLASS _____ DATE _____

SELF-EVALUATION

Listening Self-Inventory

Questions and answers about my listening	More about my answers
What kinds of music do I like to listen to?	Why do I like them?
What TV shows and movies are my favorites?	What do I like about them?
How well do I listen in school?	How much do I learn by listening?
Do I listen carefully to what my friends say?	What do I learn from them?
When is it difficult for me to listen?	What makes it difficult?
How do I use the praise and suggestions of others to improve my skills?	How do I feel about getting praise or suggestions for improvement?

PORTFOLIO ASSESSMENT

192   Holt Assessment: Writing, Listening, and Speaking

NAME _____ CLASS _____ DATE _____

SELF-EVALUATION

Speaking Self-Inventory

Questions and answers about my speaking	More about my answers
How do I feel about speaking to friends?	What do I like to discuss with them?
How do I feel about talking to adults?	Why do I feel this way?
How do I feel about reciting or speaking to the class?	Why do I feel this way?
What is the most difficult thing about speaking?	Why is it difficult?
What techniques have I learned to improve my speaking?	How do I use these techniques with friends or in class?

PORTFOLIO ASSESSMENT

Skills Profile

Student's Name _____ Grade _____

Teacher's Name _____ Date _____

For each skill, write the date the observation is made and any comments that explain the student's development toward skills mastery.

SKILL	NOT OBSERVED	EMERGING	PROFICIENT
Writing			
Writing Modes			
Write an autobiographical narrative.			
Write a short story.			
Write an expository essay analyzing a biography.			
Write an essay comparing and contrasting the ways in which different news media cover the same event.			
Write a persuasive essay.			

Skills Profile (continued)

SKILL	NOT OBSERVED	EMERGING	PROFICIENT
Write a descriptive essay.			
Write an essay analyzing a poem.			
Write an essay analyzing a short story.			
Write a research paper.			
Write a persuasive cause-and-effect essay.			
Write an essay comparing a scene from a play with its film adaptation.			
Write a business letter.			
Write the minutes of a meeting.			

Skills Profile (continued)

SKILL	NOT OBSERVED	EMERGING	PROFICIENT
Writing Process			
Prewriting			
• Choose a topic.			
• Identify purpose and audience.			
• Generate ideas and gather information about the topic.			
• Begin to organize the information.			
• Draft a thesis statement, or a sentence that expresses the main point.			
Writing a Draft			
• State the main points and include relevant support and elaboration.			

Skills Profile (continued)

SKILL	NOT OBSERVED	EMERGING	PROFICIENT
• Follow a plan of organization.			
Revising			
• Revise for content and style.			
Publishing			
• Proofread for grammar, usage, and mechanics.			
• Publish the work, or share the finished writing with readers.			
• Reflect on the writing experience.			
▶ **Listening and Speaking**			
Present an oral narrative.			

198 Holt Assessment: Writing, Listening, and Speaking

Skills Profile *(continued)*

SKILL	NOT OBSERVED	EMERGING	PROFICIENT
Debate an issue.			
Present a description.			
Present an oral interpretation of a poem.			
Present a research report.			
Deliver a persuasive speech.			
Analyze and evaluate speeches.			
Plan and organize the speech or presentation.			

Skills Profile *(continued)*

SKILL	NOT OBSERVED	EMERGING	PROFICIENT
Rehearse and deliver the presentation.			
Use effective verbal and nonverbal techniques.			
Use visual aids.			
Analyze rhetorical devices, organization, delivery, tone, and mood.			